A Measure of Success

A Measure of Success

A WOMAN'S TIMES

Edna & John Graham

To order additional copies of this book, contact:
Xlibris Corporation
1-888-795-4274
www.Xlibris.com
Orders@Xlibris.com

Contents

To my wife, Mieke Roos, who has enthusiastically supported all my attempts at writing and has brought this manuscript forward for publication with a great deal of dedication. Mieke has a spirit in tune with that of Edna Graham.

"Us girls can do amazing things when we want to."

Susan Gray (1983)

" . . . I could see traces of my mother. I can also see traces of father in Jean. I can see traces of my father in you, and I can see in Paul already traces of Daddy. I can see traces of quickness there. And I don't think we really die when the family is perpetuated."

Edna Morgan (1968)

Preface

For every Emmeline Pankhurst, for every Susan B. Anthony, there have been millions of women who have not been politically active, but who have still been progressive and led socially useful and worthwhile lives. This is the story of one of them, Edna Graham.

She grew up in a newly progressive era, just after World War I. Then, women were beginning to find their independent feet. Being "in-service" was no longer an acceptable "career", when women were being employed in men's roles during war time, and when at last a young girl might have her own aspirations. There was even a questioning of the complete reliance on a husband.

She was drawn, by force of circumstance, towards a career in nursing. It was possible to get training in nursing even though she had left school too early, and it did involve helping others, so nursing became her goal. Yet, force of other circumstances foiled her attempt. First it was sickness of the body, then sickness of the heart. Her marriage forced her back into the age-old role of wife and mother, a supporter of her husband, and eventually a widow.

Had she failed then? There were other wives, mothers and women in careers, who made steady progress towards an independent role and stature, and who achieved their targets. Were they successes while she failed?

How do you measure the value of a life: if she had tried but failed? If she had failed in her goal but succeeded as a mother in raising a healthy family? Is that success or "failure"? Did she help any other women in making their goals? What is the measure of success? The answers are not clear but this is her story.

First there is a young girl and a woman, struggling for her independence from her family, and from the restraints of it in this way. She had no grand plan other than that she wanted to nurse. And she did nurse, enough to show that she had talent and capability, but when confronted with a love OR a career (Robert was too old fashioned to have tolerated a working wife in those days) she was a woman too much in love.

So she became wife and mother: a member of a family group. Through her own personality she helped to shape those traits and behavioral patterns, which are parts of the family inheritance. She took the experience of prior generations, enhanced and enriched it, before passing it on to her own children and their children. She added her humour, her curiosity, her interest in others, her industry and even her biases (good and bad), to the stability of working ancestors.

We are such a compilation of origins, of in-born intelligence, of others' likes and dislikes, of understandings learned and inherited, and of ingrained characteristics; it amazes that so much differs when so much remains the same. We seem different. It takes the perspective of the years to see the repetitions of personality that belie the differences.

Edna was a link in the family chain, a strong tie between the past and the future. This is her story, and the fact that it is worth telling IS a measure of success.

There was nothing atypical about Edna. The strength of her story is that it was SO typical of many thousands of women in her time. You may recognize your own mother or even yourself in part – you are meant to.

In 1996 Edna sat with her son, John, and recounted the story of her life while a tape recorder revolved for posterity. They spent six hours over the story. The story bubbled with repetition and laughing but occasionally it brought tears too. You may even be able to recognize the Welsh dialect and idiom in her enthusiastic English. She hesitates and terminates sentences with a lot of meaning. Seventeen years later I typed her words verbatim to ensure their survival, and realized that there was a story worth telling. Thus, this book is told largely by Edna (her own words are inset in italics), with explanations, footnotes and final chapters added by John. Nothing has been invented. To the best of our knowledge the story is entirely factual.

Emmy Roos scanned an early dot-matrix printed version of this text and painstakingly produced a

WORD file having had to correct almost every word in the optical character recognition version. Without her work, the words of Edna Graham would not be reaching you today in printed form.

John Graham

Chapter 1

Early Years

E dna Morgans lived in the first two thirds of the twentieth century. She was Welsh.

"I was born by Red Lion Street on June 3rd, 1901-It was an old manse amongst a lot of small houses . . . an old manse, an old vicarage . . . yes I suppose it was a vicarage adjoining a lot of little tiny smaller houses. NO . . . it may not have been a manse. A vicar owned it. No, it wasn't detached house. My Father was allowed to have it on condition he let the vicar's daughter and her friend live there. They were two missionaries from India or Africa. They weren't there all the time; they went back, you see. A Miss Evans and a Miss Holmgren . . . So we had a harmonium there and they used to have services. The services were held in a sort of front room, the best room only used for visitors. The services were for the public, and the house was in an area nearby the Whitehall public house and the Corbett Hotel, quite near, in a poorer

15

*area of the town. No, we weren't born in the atmo-
sphere of the pubs . . . we were with the missionaries, and with the harmonium. The harmonium
played a bigger part in our house than anything.
Later on we all went to it, you see."*

The town was Towyn, in Meirionythshire, on the
far west coast of Wales, separated from England by
the bulk of the central mountains topped by Cader
ldris. The town is now called Tywyn in a flurry of mid-
twentieth century Welsh nationalism, but even at the
turn of the century it catered for English tourists on
its sandy beach. It was as far from England as one
could get, yet it was not as Welsh as the upland farm
communities. The inhabitants of Towyn knew of the
outside world . . . even if foreign parts did need good
Welsh missionaries for their salvation.

Nevertheless, Towyn was a quiet unchanging seaside town, which today remains very much as it did
at the turn of the century.

The Morgans family was the usual size for the
turn of the century: large with ten siblings, so most
family activities meant involving a lot of bodies.

*"My Father was a builder. I remember moving
before I was six. I remember the furniture having
gone and the last portions going. I was coming
home from school, skipping down the hill. Down
the hill, running down the hill, ever such a steep
hill . . . running around the corner into a handcart
that my Father had. That's how we went to our
new home in 'Maesnewydd' down by the beach. I
talked and talked and talked how he was going
with this handcart to my friends."*

*"One of my friends lived in one of the little
houses nearby, next to us. Her name was Ethel
Jones, one of a family of thirteen. They lived in*

16

such a small house; only two bedrooms there, one room downstairs and an annex which was a back kitchen-cum-everything. I honestly don't know . . . I never used to know how they slept."

"We were ten. We weren't all there when we moved because some were away. I was the eighth . . . my eldest brother Llewellyn, Elizabeth Margaretta . . . I'm giving their full names . . . Jane Mary, Sophie . . . Sophia her name was. She wasn't Sophie-Ann. She put on Ann afterwards. Now there was John James, David Thomas . . . David Thomas was named after twins, as my Father was one of twins . . . and Maria."

The Morgans Family

"She also added Annie Maria on her name. She was Maria. My name is Edna, but I also added Edna May because Edna May was an actress, you see. Now we come to William Richard. He had two names. Then Albert Emrys had two names and he was the youngest of all."

"I remember going on top of a lot of things on a handcart, and Willie and Emrys, and we were *wheeled all the way down to the beach. My Father was pushing us. He had built, or was in the act of building, a new marine terrace. By the time our house was built, the second had been built and he was in the process of finishing the second and building the third."*

"We were looking forward to the move. We had all bricks and we had a field, and we had planks. We had a wonderful childhood really. The house, 'Maesnewydd', was the first one at the end of the road. Down the field we had seesaws, and we had to make them out of . . . But there was one place we hadn't got to go. It was a lime-pit, where they mixed the lime, and it was fenced off. We were never to go near it. We never did. We went round it, because we knew it would burn. At the end Dadda also had a shed, and in this shed were all his tools. He had ladders. These ladders and the wood he was building with were all placed up so that they could season. The ladders were flat. We weren't allowed to touch the ladders."

The lessons were well learnt, to have such meaning from a perspective of 60 years further on. How frustrating it must have been to a little one . . . not to touch the ladders. The large family had a span of 19 years, so it was self-regulating. Discipline was not just a parental stricture. Dadda and Mamma were special.

"By trade really he was a plasterer, but he was also a builder and contractor. He had started and worked his trade, becoming a plasterer in Liverpool, many years before, of course. He was Welsh, from Towyn, born in Erw Porthed, a farm. They had to leave the farm because of foot-and-mouth disease."

"My Mother was born, also Welsh, between Ruthlan and Rhyl in North Wales, you see. Now

*she had lost her parents at eight and she had gone
to Liverpool. Now, my Father served his appren-
ticeship under her brother. He was working on
Liverpool Cathedral, but that was many years before, well before they were married. Now wait a
minute . . . my elder sister, Gretta's 17 years older
than me, and I was born in 1901, and they were
two years married before they had her. It was about
1880 or thereabouts."*

*"Well, Dadda's boss had to go to hospital. Any-
way, he liked his boss, so he went to see his boss in
hospital, and they were only allowed in strictly two-
by-two to see him. A young lady went in to see him,
and she sat on one side of the bed, and Dadda sat
on the other side of the bed. Mamma told me
'. . . and of course he was Dadda you see. And he
came to see my eldest brother, and, of course, he
took me home.' Mamma used to say that. 'You know
you had to have an introduction . . . 'and . . . 'Of
course he took me home.' She always used to end
like that. She was very funny, my Mother was, you
know."*

Edna Morgans was not destined to become a
Welsh nationalist — the early 1900's were not a time
for nationalism — there was not enough time for
idealism, and the war that came early in her life was
an English war. Furthermore, there was little need
to PROVE oneself different from the English; the
difference between the moneyed holidaymaker and
the children of the town was obvious. The Morgans
family anyway had strong connections with Liverpool,
the closest large English city. Yet the family WAS
Welsh despite its Liverpuddlian start.

*"In Liverpool they lived in Garston. Llew and
Gretta were born in Liverpool. Because their*

neighbours and everyone spoke English to them, after Llew was born, my Father decided to come home to Towyn to look after his father. His father by then had lost his farm because they had no recompense at all (for foot-and-mouth disease). He had become a coal merchant with the rest of the money. So now he was delivering coal and my Father thought he ought to go and look after his father who was 72, and lived in Frankwell Street. So I think Jane Mary, Sophie, John James, and Thomas were all born in Frankwell Street, Maria and I and Willie and Emrys were born in Red Lion Street."

"Red Lion Street . . . there was no Red Lion pub. Now it's Queen Street. The Queen came through Towyn from Dolgelley. She came through the very smallest street and went up the hill past the school, and now it's called Queen Street. Even now though if I write to my same friend who is living in my old home, I write '5, Red Lion Street', and it gets delivered. I think Red Lion Street is much prettier than Queen's Street."

There is stability in a small town. Life evolves very slowly, and not at the bidding of the powers that be. It takes more than a Royal decree to change a place name.

The Welsh don't all speak Welsh, the language is curious hodge podge of ancient Celtic consonants, and rhythmic vowels, mixed with Saesneg Cymraeg. When a Welsh word doesn't exist, an English one is given a Welsh ending . . . Saesneg, the language of the tourists, is converted into Cymraeg — Welsh.

Yet, there is a pride in Wales for the tongue, lately revived after years of English dominance. In days long since gone, Red Lion Street, when it was a footpath, might have had a welsh name, but the Welsh have come to live with bilingually, so the English name isn't strange. Yet, it might change soon to Welsh again, perhaps to Stryd Llew Goch.

In large families, there was usually one or two early entries into the family bible, one or two small graves on the Welsh hillside. The Morgans were no exception. John James Morgans is well remembered:

"I was six years of age, and I was just going to school, the Council School. But one of the happiest memories I have is . . . John James was six years older than me . . . I remember going to school on his shoulders, being carried to school. He stuttered a bit. He used to bend down. He was only twelve . . . he died at twelve. I remember going to school on my brother's shoulders, being picked up . . . he had very very fair curly hair and I remember it quite distinctly. He died of double pneumonia."

"You see at twelve years of age he was frightened of a teacher. He had pneumonia on one side first, and while he was lying in his bed ill he was so frightened of not attending school with this Maud Evans. She was a terror; she was really, all through her life, a terror. She used to frighten the life out of the children. One day, my Mother goes up with a drink for him and she misses Jack. Jack had gone out of bed, and he'd run out of the front door in his fever, and he had run to the end of the road. They found him at the top in a high state of fever and when he came back . . . remember he was only twelve . . . he was carried back, and he had a double dose of it, and he died."

"When we heard that Jack had died, we all had to go and see him. The little girl from next door to 'Maesnewydd' . . . Mona Barnett — was his sweetheart, and I remember standing seeing Jack in his coffin, and I saw his little schoolgirl

21

sweetheart come in there and putting a red rose on him. I remember seeing Jack's very fair hair quite well . . . and after that we went out."

"Now, I don't think I went to school, but I met a friend. I'm sure she must have been Ethel Jones. Or Maggie Barbara, you see (chuckles), and I re-member saying " . . . and we're going to have horses and carts, horses and proper carriages, you know, proper horses and carriages. You see, I was between six and seven, and I remember bragging how we were going to the funeral. And thinking how we were going to be very high up in the coaches and she had to look for me high up."

"The hearse was in front of us, I remember quite well, and we used to stand quite still (softly) when we saw this hearse. The local railway porter drove it. He had two black horses. They were lovely horses. There were other horses, one horse at a time, that took this carriage in, and I remember looking up. I wasn't a bit perturbed about the funeral re-ally. But I remember looking out to see if they were looking at me, you see. I remember looking out both sides and I never saw them all the way there."

"We had to go up to the cemetery and I remem-ber a wonderful thing there. My brother, John James, Jack we used to call him, was a singer. He was always singing, and always happy, and always kind. If I ever cried he would sing. He would sit with you and sing. I was a crier. I believe I was the worst crier of the family, (laughter). I remember the tears rolling down my face and being as wet as anything and watching Jack . . . and he'd say "P— p—p – put me amongst the girls, am—mongst the girls," and by the time he had sung that one or two times . . . we'd all be laughing."

"Eventually we'd all go up on the settle be-hind the long table. My Father had a long farm-yard table and this was scrubbed white. But he had made a settle at the back of it. A settle was *made in the form of a sofa, but it had woods (slats) across, you see. It was not padded. No, no, it was padded with just cushions. But if you went underneath, if you were in a bad temper, as I often was — you could go underneath (giggles) those things, and push them out, you see! And if anyone sat in one of them, and you'd forgotten to put it back in its groove well you sat through it, didn't you? And when YOU sit through one of those . . . (giggling) your legs are up. And Father sitting there . . . There was Willie, Emrys and I. We'd sit always on that side with Mamma and Dadda by us, you see. And I would have to sit between the two boys. Well, you can just imagine the time I had . . . not pleasant sometimes it wasn't I tell you, because the two boys were . . . err . . . They would egg me on to anything and I would be the one to do it, you see, and I would be the one to get the smacking. But it was a wonderful happy time, really, when I think back about it. But old Jack would always get us on there. Jack was a nice lad. I would say that he would have grown up like Llew: really gentle. He wasn't rough."*

"I'll tell you a little tale about Jack. At the end of the road where my Father was building, there was a gentleman there by the name of Captain Preston. He had retired (from the sea). He'd got one, two, three sons and a daughter, as far as I remember. But I remember Alfred Preston was the same age as Jack, and there was another boy . . . younger. Now Thomas was a fighter. Jack was a peacemaker. Now Jack came in all blood one day. But he hadn't been fighting; he'd been in-between Leonard Preston and Thomas, Tom his brother, fighting. The one that came in bloody was poor old Jack. But he was pushing Tom home from the fight, you see, so he had the knocks from Leonard Preston."

"Funny thing, you know, even today (fifty years

on) Maria went to Aberdovey, and she went to Polyngwyn, nearby our home in Maesnewydd there, right on top of the mountain . . . and on the top of Polyngwyn, she met a man. She looked at this man and said 'Excuse me, you remind me of somebody I know, by the name of . . . ' and she named the eldest son of this Preston. He said 'I am that man'. What a funny thing . . . life goes on."

Edna's playmates in the family circle were boys, and her activities were inevitably theirs, and masculine, when she was small. Perhaps that gave her some of the strength she needed later.

"Now then, Alfred Preston, and Captain Preston, they lived in a house encircled with stone walls, you see. Thomas and Jack would go and play with Alfred, and his brother. Well, where Jack was, I used to want to go. I wasn't allowed in the doorway though, you see."

"Now Willie, Emrys and I, we found that if we went round the end of our garden, and went along the hedge there, we knew a place where we could put our feet. So one would be pushing the other, and invariably it was I being pushed up. I remember quite well (giggling) being pushed up, and I turned around and said 'I can see them . . . I can see them.' I had glasses. I was the only one with glasses, and I remember falling right over the wall and my glasses were in bits. By this time the boys couldn't come because I was supposed to sit on top of the wall to pull them up you see. They were shouting . . . I said 'I don't know. I broke my glasses. I broke my glasses.' But I managed to get back somehow . . . "

Schools in rural Wales, at the start of this century were good at the elementary level. There was little difference between the education of girls and boys though they were separated for cookery and wood-work, and for different sports. The real separation came later. Only a small proportion of children went forward to University level, and very few of those were girls. The girls were mainly offered only what would now be called Liberal Arts . . . languages, history, and biology.

Edna enjoyed school, and was good at her studies. It was her enthusiasm that got her into trouble with authorities.

> *"Yes, I loved school, until I lost . . . You see, if you went to our school . . . Yes, I loved school really — parts of it. I ran away at fourteen, because I decided . . ."*
>
> *"When I went into the little school first . . . Now I must have been ten, before scholarship year. Nine I was. If you attended for five years you qualified for a gold watch, but during that time I had to have attention for my eyes, and I had to go to Shrewsbury. Now I was very grieved. I missed three halves, a full day and another half-day (in five years) and I missed my gold watch. Then I sort of . . ."Oh, Blow it . . . "*

Whenever the subject of schooldays came up, thirty, forty, or fifty years later, it was never long before Eric Lloyd was mentioned.

> *"I was always running off to meet my school friends, and of those school friends I had one main friend — a boy called Eric Lloyd. I knew I could always come home with him. He was quiet. I could do just what I liked with him."*
>
> *"He used to be responsible for his two brothers and a sister, who was little, you see. Delys Tlws*

25

Vaughan Lewis Lloyd! Later she became an announcer on the radio. She wasn't 'Tlws' (pretty); she was a rather bad tempered little madam. Now there were Wyn and Alvernon, and everyone had four or five names — even 'Eric Vaughan Lewis Lloyd.' Vaughan after his mother Vaughan, Lewis and Lloyd after Dr. Lloyd."

There are very few Welsh surnames in the country: Jones, Williams, Hughes, Thomas, Owen, Roberts, Morgans, Davies, Lewis, Lloyd, Griffiths, Jenkins, Rees, Evans and Tudor. Welsh first names were also few and they included variants of the surnames, just as Lewis had been transformed for Eric Lloyd. Thus William Williams, Evan Evans, and Owen Owen all figured among my acquaintances. Since there were so few surnames there had to be ways of distinguishing between the various Mrs. Williams's and Mr. Jones's. In school, everyone knew TH taught chemistry, C taught French and RR taught mathematics and history. They were respectively Mr. T.H. Jones, Miss C. Jones and Mr. R.R. Jones. On the other hand our neighbour was Roberts Esgidia since he kept the shoe (esgid) shop, and Mr. Roberts Glyddyn and Mr. Roberts Glyddyn Uchaf were two farmers owning neighbouring farms called Glyddyn and Glyddyn Uchaf: Glyddyn Uchaf (higher) being a little higher in the valley. They were not related.

Likewise, a father's profession could distinguish children. Huwcyn Chem's father was the chemist. Thus, having five names already was a distinctive advantage to any Welsh child, even though they were shortened quickly.

"Now Eric would walk home with me, and Eric was more my . . . Whatever I told poor Eric to

do, he'd do it. If I said 'Put your hand in there, there's red currents in there', he'd bend down and do it. One day, we were behind the police station. I said 'For currents . . . PUSH' I said and he wasn't . . . 'Push, harder . . . push your hand in Eric. Go on, get away! Let me do it', and I pushed right in, with my hand on the red current bushes, and my hand grabbed at the bushes! (laughing)"

"I never said a word, you know . . . but a voice, a huge gruff voice comes . . . 'Now you. Come right on in' he said. He picked that bunch of . . . You come right in and bring it to the police station.' So dutifully, Eric went to the police station. He was a doctor's son. I wasn't so obedient. I would have run! He wouldn't run (laughing), so we better go. So we were landed in the police station only to be offered a whole dish full of red currents. I never ate a red current after. I hated the sight of red currents after that."

Food was simpler in the country at the turn of the century, and in retrospect it was certainly healthier than our now easy ability to open a bottle or a can of whatever. Nevertheless, children don't change, sweet and sticky food was (and is) hunted down.

"We had another skidaddle with Eric. After school, we'd run all the way home for dinner, mind you, Mamma would cook a nice big cabbage for us. The day we had a cabbage for dinner, we'd have a lot of butter on it. We didn't always have potatoes, you know, we had cabbage. Another good dinner we had that I liked better than anything. We had potatoes put in a basin, and we had to crush them with a fork and we had buttermilk put on them."

"Before we could have that buttermilk and potatoes I had to go to Sir Hayden Jones' farm for the

27

buttermilk. I had a sort of arrangement with my maths master (he wouldn't be called an arithmetic master there) that I would give him a bottle full. He would give me a penny for the bottleful. But the whole can only cost a ha'penny. (Giggles.) It had a lid on, you see, and if you poured it out into this lid it also had a spout on and I could fill his bottle, and I'd carry that bottle and the can. I'd pour a drop in that thing and I'd have a jolly good drink before I started home. More often than not it was HALF full before I arrived home. I'd go home . . . well, It was a big can to me then. (Giggles) But we'd have buttermilk and potatoes. That was a lovely dinner."

"And off we'd run to school again. Now we'd come home one way, and go back another way: we had a jolly good roundabout. Coming home past the toy railway, we would go back the other way. When we went back the other way, we would perhaps meet different friends, you see, and by going up the hill with them, they might have had sweets. We never had money for sweets. I remember asking my Father once for a penny to go for some chips . . . the chip shop had just opened . . . but he said 'I haven't got any, I haven't got any money'. I don't think we ever bothered to go for them really. We had a lollipop shop at the bottom (of the hill) she who made her own toffee; we had real good toffee. We used to go in there. For a ha'penny, we could have a big bag full of these rolled up little treacle toffees, and when you got hold them, even the paper was sticky . . . but oh, that delicious taste when you were hungry!"

"I'll tell you one thing. When we went home at teatime, you see, we'd go the top way. We'd be running home and somehow or other that journey was nothing, we'd be sort of just skipping all the way. We were skipping all the way home. We had one job we had to do some times on the way home, if we *had taken the bread to the bakehouse . . . My Mother would make bread. This was baked by the local baker. She would make the dough and put it in a clean pillowslip. This clean pillowslip was out in a little handcart that my Father made. Just two wheels and a handle. Whoever took it to the baker, the other one brought it back home teatime. You see it was lovely feeling when you knew it was your time to bring the bread home, because you could have a bite. You never bit the dough, did you?! We had two lots — we had brown bread, brown barley bread, barley my Father grew in his field (it wasn't real barley, it was barley and wheat mixed) . . . and then we'd have the white bread. One white loaf of bread, and God Help us if we touched the white loaf. (That bread was for visitors.) But we didn't mind, any hard crust would do; we used to bite a big lot of it, you see . . ."*

Years later, Edna's son did almost the same thing. Collecting bread during wartime meant handing in ration coupons and still biting off the corner of fresh soft bread in the hope that it might not be noticed.

Schooling in Wales was quite formal. The framework defined the subjects to be taught to provide the basic life skills of reading, writing, and arithmetic. The standard of education however depended on the individual teacher and here Edna seems to have been lucky. Her buttermilk-loving Mathematics master was innovative.

"Wait a minute now then, when I was about nine, this maths master picked about five from the class, and we all had to stand in the front. We were the ones who really could make a box best in that class. He used to teach us how to shape boxes and how to get to measure for them, and how to do

29

the little grooves so one (side) fixed into the other.
Well, we were all standing in the front, and there
were only two girls of us, and I was one of them. I
was as proud as Lucifer, you know. I had a feeling
that the buttermilk helped a bit (laughter). Any-
way, Mr. Hughes, he was a man I liked, you see.
There was a girl called Bythig Hughes, who WAS
clever, and me. Then there was a boy called Huw
Chem. Huw 'Chemist' we used to call him. Huwcyn
Chem, Huw Jones 'Chemist' . . . and he was a
clever boy. Then there was Marshall Lloyd, son of
the solicitor. Of course he could do no wrong, you
see, but he had the most funny pinchy writing you
ever saw . . . I mimicked his writing for years. Just
when I was really vindictive to him, I would say
'Look how you're writing'. You know he'd crushed
it in — it was like his whole nature. But anyway,
Eric and I were standing by each other, and they
told us we had to go to a class up. Remember, I'd
missed quite a long time out of class, and accord-
ing to home, I was supposed to be a dullard. Now,
I went up to this next class, and we were trying for
the scholarship."

The 'Scholarship' was also called the 11+ examination. It was a major hurdle for British schoolchildren until being abandoned in the seventies. After
attending infants' and elementary schools, each
child, at 11 years of age, took a national examination. The results of this examination determined
whether the youngster would go on into the County
(later called the Grammar) School or into the Sec-
ondary Modern School. The difference? Those in
the County or Grammar (Yr Ysgol Ramadeg) had a
chance to progress to college, while those in Sec-
ondary Modern were given more practical instruc-
tion (woodworking, metal shop, cooking, etc) to fit

them for early entry into non-academic life. The scholarship was the major division in the educational road, which in some cases doomed children to a laboring life, when as late bloomers they could have done well in university.

"Now the day of the result came. You can just imagine me running across the road . . . we used to have our results outside the post-office. That was on the right-hand side of the street, and the doctor lived on the left-hand side. He lived in a big house, this doctor's son, Eric, did. I just looked at the results and I ran across the road. I pulled Eric out of his house. They were just-so people they were. (They said grace and everything, they did. You had to be quiet at the table.) We ran across the road, as quick as we could, and I said 'What do you think? What do you think, Eric?' 'I don't know, I don't know.' Poor old Eric! 'What do you think? I've beaten you!' We five were on the top of the list. That's what amused me. Although we'd been transferred from the second class to the higher class, we were the TOP of the list. It was Huwcyn 'Chem' at the top, Bythig Hughes the next, Marshal Lloyd in the next and then Edna Morgans in the next and Eric Lloyd at the next. I was glad we came in that way, really. We didn't do badly. That was the scholarship results when I suppose we were between 10 and 11. But we didn't know anything about these months and birthdays or anything, really. We never thought about it. We were too happy. We were always happy."

"We went on to the County School. There was a bachelor headmaster there, who was extremely stern . . . Tom Jones. He got his degree after he became headmaster. He was a marvelous fellow. Well, we all went there."

"That first day at the County School we had

*boater hats. I had a head of very frizzy hair. It's
been the bane of my life all my life. I was very fond
of going into the sea, and Father was the one who
combed the salt out. Oh, it was always luggy, it
was never right. But anyway, now, it was properly
done that day and I had this board hat on. I had a
big boater hat, fairly wide, and it had a brown
and gold band on it. It was the proper badge and
we had a brown gym-slip sort of thing . . . and off
we went to school."*

*"But could I keep this hat on. . . ?! The wind
blew, and it fell, and fell, and fell, until it landed
on the back of my neck going to school that first
day. Of course, all the others were there, but I was
quite comfortable. There was elastic in the front
and I was so comfortable. I never even thought
about my hat being on my head. Then somebody
said 'What is your name?' 'Edna Morgans.' 'Will
you put your hat on'. It was one of the mistresses.
(Shirley) 'Will you put your hat on.' From that
time onwards, that hat was a nuisance, it never
stuck there. Oh, they were very severe."*

*"I'll tell you one thing — when I walked round
that school for the first time, how pleased I was
that my Father had had a hand in the building. I
was an awfully conceited girl about my Father really. My father was to me a . . . more . . . I idolised
what he did in Towyn. You know, idolised him I
think because I heard that he went to school late in
life . . . and I was going round the school . . ."*

Fifty years later, another little girl, due eventually to be Edna's daughter in law, knew that her Father had invented television. She was quite firm that
the one he had constructed and which was now in
the attic was the first of a kind. In fact, he was a television enthusiast and he mended them in his spare
time. Children need to believe in their fathers.

"*You all (we all) had to go for . . . what do you call it? . . . 'Prayers', into the central hall. It was a smart school, it was. We all had to hang these hats on certain pegs in this porch before we went in. The girls had to go one side and the boys had to go the other side, and I looked where Eric was. Hoping he wasn't very far away, you see. (Giggles) Well, anyway we all went to the central hall. When I went in there of course we landed in the front, didn't we, and on a proper raised platform in front of us were all the headmaster (and staff). There was Tom Jones, whom I remember very very clearly. There was Joseph Jones, and the Geography mistress. There was the French mistress, and Morris 'Latin', who was I'm sure 6 foot 6 . . . there were lots more than this. Then there was a man I loved very much. There was the English master, Mr. T.V. Davies. He was extremely nice looking, and every face went to him. He smiled. He wasn't severe. He was right through his life like that.*"

"*Now Morris Latin of course, l-e-a-n-e-d. He leant. He didn't stand ever. He used to lean usually on either the back of the platform or he'd lean on a wall by the side of him. When we were saying prayers, we'd be looking around and we'd be whispering (sotto voice) to each other 'Look at old Morris Latin, I bet he's near Miss Evans French.' She was as small as he was tall.*"

"*Now then, we had our classes. Well, I liked French. I thought French was absolutely IT when I went home. The first day I learnt French, they put a house in a picture on the board, and they called it a 'maison'. I think I was always keen on anything to do with a house. I'm sure I'd have learnt French through a house, because my play books as a child were everything to do with building houses . . . I used to know how to draw a window, I used to know how to draw a range, when I was*"

*quite young. When I went into the cookery
class . . . Miss Owen Cookery, oh, we didn't like
her at all. She never seemed to come into 'Prayers'
— she never was in 'Prayers'. She evidently was
preparing the lesson . . . poor woman . . . the more
I think of her . . . she was very stern. They were
all stern. But anyway, the French class I liked. I
liked Miss Evans, Geography. I got on all right,
fine . . . but what did disturb me was Morris Latin.
I never not anymore than 7% in that thing. I
couldn't do Latin. I could NOT memorise."*

Edna also could NOT stay out of trouble. Lively
spirits cannot.

*"(Giggles) Now, I was happy . . . I was always
happy. There were only six girls in our form, only
six: there was Bythig Hughes, myself, Irene Williams, Twina Williams, Nell Porthgwyn, and . . . I
was in the second row. The six girls were on one
side and there were a lot of boys in our class. Who
should be sitting in front of me but Irene Williams, who was the daughter of a minister. She wore
her hair in nice neat plaits. But I saw something
on her hair and it made me laugh, you see. I looked
at my companion, who was Bythig Hughes, and
made her laugh. And I looked back; it was (she
spoke quietly) a louse from her hair. We could see
this thing going down on the plait. Now I'd always envied those plaits until I found this thing
coming down. After that I didn't mind the boys
pulling my hair because I knew there weren't any
of those things creeping down in it (laughing)."*

*"I can see Morris Latin leaning on the board
as usual. I could always see a very funny side of
anything, doesn't matter what had happened. Well,
I was laughing at this, and Bythig laughed and
laughed. 'Edna Morgans, come out,' he said. So I*

came out, and he gave me a punishment: a detention. If you had detention three nights a week it meant you had to go in on Saturday morning, and that Saturday my mother was coming home. During that time, my Mother was in London with my sister Sophie who always seemed to be ill and my Mother always had an emergency call. So I knew I couldn't (miss Saturday) . . ."

"Still I had to go to detention, which is an hour after school, before I went home. 'Who sent you in?' We'd all sit there in detention and the man who was the master allocated for the week would come and say 'What are you here for Edna Morgans?' 'I've been sent by Mr. Morris Latin for an hour's detention for three nights, Sir.' Standing up by my seat as good as gold, you know. 'Your name's not on the book. Go on home.' Well, by Jove, my name's not on the book. So I went home."

"He had (also) given me a whole book to translate into Latin. If I could have guessed it into English it would have been all right, but to translate it back into Latin was awful. Well, I said 'Yes Sir. Yes Sir. Yes Sir' and I went home that day as meek and mild. I never stole a bike, jumped on anybody else's bike. I never ran. My hat was on the right angle. I walked home and I sat. You see, there was no Mother there and I sat in the back parlour. In our back parlour at Maesnwydd there was a bit book case . . . open, mind you. I sat wondering how to translate this thing. Well, I sat in front looking idly around, at this cupboard at home, you se, and lo and behold, I see a book identical to the one I'd got in my hand. (Excitedly) But it was the whole translation of the book! In Latin! So I just sat down there and then and I wrote the whole blooming book out that night. It wasn't a very big book, you know, but it seemed to me big. I wrote it all up."

"So the next night I again went to the detention.

*'Your name isn't down, off you go.' So off I run.
The third time it happened, 'No, your name
isn't . . . now off you go. You know very well, your
name is not down.' So I didn't go on Saturday
morning, but Monday morning came and it was
our lesson. 'Well, Edna Morgans?' 'Yes, Sir' 'Have
you finished?' 'Yes, Sir.' 'Bring it up here.' 'Yes,
Sir.' I was ever so serious, you know. (Laughing) I
hadn't told a soul that I'd copied it. I went up
there, stood in front of him. He looked at me. He
had a wicked look in his eye and he said 'How did
you do this?' 'I copied it, Sir.' 'On you,' he said
and he just knocked me on the head 'Go and sit
down,' I went to sit down."*

*"What made me leave you ask? Well, I'll tell
you what made me leave. It was my third year there.
What really upset me in that school was not the
Latin class at all. What upset me was the cookery
class. I'd gone to cookery lesson and in the olden
days they didn't deal with you like they do today.
You had a lot of seats, which you brought forward:
you did have a sort of a bench, but sometimes you
sat there without a bench. There was a bench this
time in front of us, a sort of long table bench it
was, and we were sitting there. There was a pig's
picture on the wall, you see. The cookery mistress
was teaching us the joints of the pigs. Now it came
to the rump and I whispered 'Paham hi nid yn
galw o y tin y foch? Bythig Hughes.' I said 'Why
didn't she call it the pig's bottom'. She laughed
and I laughed."*

*"'Edna Morgans. Go out of the room until
you apologise.' So I dutifully went out of the room
and stood in the corridor. I completely forgot that
she'd told me to apologise. In fact, I don't think I
knew what it meant then, really. Well, somehow or
other the time passed very quickly in that little corridor. There were lots of things on the wall, and I
was always happy even if I could draw a design*

on the wall. I was always drawing in my own way. I was quite happy and I just waited until the class finished, about an hour and a half later. They were very hard at it. All the class filed out, and one girl, Twina Williams (she was of the old class before I'd gone up), she said 'You're silly, you're in for it, my girl. Why didn't you go and say you're sorry at once?' 'Oh Crikey! Was that all she wanted? Oh, I'll go and say I'm sorry', I said. So off I went in now to say I was sorry. I went in and I said 'I'm sorry, Miss Owen.' 'Don't you dare come in and say you're sorry' she said to me. 'Leave my class.' So I just left it and ran home. I wouldn't go back to school after that for all the money in the world. I ran away from school."

(It didn't seem very terrible) "No, it didn't, but, I went home. The next day, I wouldn't go to school. 'No, I'm not going. She told me to go home' I said. So I just stayed home and by this time everyone was thinking I was bad. I didn't think I was bad. She'd told me to do it, and this time I was going to do what she told me. So I said 'No, I'm not going.' Do you know, during the morning, who should come to the house but the headmaster? 'No, I'm not coming to school' 'Well, you're not going to try it?' 'No, I'm not coming to school' I said. 'She told me to get out and I'm going to stay out'. I was stuck by the door, so if my Mother drew me to him, I was going to run. I was standing there. He said 'Do you know,' he said to my Mother, 'do you know this girl is just as clever as her brother?'"

"I'd always grown up with Willie. Willie could do everything, and I could do nothing. I was always in trouble. He was never. He was the one who pushed me on. NOW I realise, being as old as I am and seeing what has happened, that that was part of his character, to get you into trouble. That was part of his illness, but we didn't know at the time. I was always in trouble and he was not. I

always broke my glasses, he never had any glasses to break, you see. "

William Morgans was later to graduate with high honours in Mathematics and Physics, to take part in British Expeditionary explorations, to become a double Doctor of Science and Law as a result, and to die . . . in a mental asylum. Now he was just Edna's clever brother.

"Well, now I refused to go to school. I was old enough to leave. 14 years I was. 'Well, you're foolish.' 'I'm not going to school. I'm going to nurse'. I always did want to become a nurse. So I suppose to my loss I left school then. My Mother and Father tried to talk me back to going to school, but I never went back to school after that experience; not once. I left. My Father and Mother never forced us to do anything. I always had in my mind, that doesn't matter what happened, I was going to become a nurse."

Leaving school at fourteen was permissible, yet Edna was clearly academically bright having gained a year in school and still having come fifth in the scholarship county 11+ examination. Her parents didn't force her to continue in school or go to college. When she left, in what was really a fit of pique, neither was she much encouraged to seek a career – staying at home to scrub floors and make the beds, or to labor on a relative's farm without pay, was quite acceptable. It would have been different, very different, had she been a boy. Hopefully today it would be different also for the girl.

Chapter 2

Directions

I n times past in Britain, higher education was limited to boys. In the upper class there had been a strict hierarchy: the eldest son and heir was trained to support his inheritance (even by University education if need be); the second son served His (or Her) Majesty in the army (or navy) and the third went into the church. Later sons took their chances in commerce perhaps. Girls however were trained in the social graces. Their destiny was to marry: to manage a household through its staff and to host their husband's friends. Below the upper classes, finances limited how far families could emulated this scheme.

However, emancipation had already begun in the 19th century. There were two professions open to women: nursing and teaching. Florence Nightingale's example in the Crimea in 1858 made nursing a heroic activity and suitable for women (though the doctor's role was still a male domain). The teaching woman had developed from infant teaching to elementary and college ranks, though senior teaching posts for women were still only available in teaching women and girls. Thus, Edna's elder sisters had been able to move into these careers: Jane Mary and, later, Margretta into teaching, and Sophie and Maria into nursing.

However being last in the family, Edna appeared condemned to stay at home to help her Mother to keep home for the elder family members, and for summer visitors. At best, she might graduate to an 'in-service' post for a better-off family . . . with a long life of cleaning drudgery for a pittance. This direction was made more probable now that her apparently bright intelligence and scholarly ability was nullified by a fit of pique in leaving school.

There are so many directions open to a young mind: some weak, some strong, some possible and others impossible. Quitting school at 14 quickly eliminated directions leading to a higher education, and being at the tail end of a large family appeared to confirm her menial prospects. But even for that a young girl needed training.

"During this time my Mother and I were very happy together. I was working hard at home. There was plenty of work at home. I was learning to scrub and do everything at home, make meals, and so on. I never knew I was learning to do anything, because my Mother never forced me to do anything. She'd say 'I think we'd better wash the back kitchen

today', or she would be washing and somehow or other I'd picked up a floor cloth. I used to wash the back kitchen without knowing what I did."

"Then she'd tell me to go and hang out the clothes. 'Now, hang them on the gorse bushes', and I hung them all on the gorse bushes. They were supposed to take something green from the gorse bushes to make them white. That's all I knew. Oh, she never hung them on the line. If she had anything that didn't come as white as it should do, she would put it on the grass, and I would be allowed to go when it was dry, take a bucket of water and throw it over the washing. But it had to remain on the grass. The big sheets or things like that, she would put properly on the line. I knew years ago that when you hang out clothes on a gorse bush that it was supposed to take something, a sort of a bleaching. We were never allowed to bring them in, even if it rained. It was supposed to get whiter. Remember, it was very clear air, and what's more, our gorse bushes weren't behind the houses, they were in the field."

But Edna liked children and another of life's directions, which she favoured, was one involving small children:

"I wanted to become a children's nurse first. Going about with children, just to push the pram, sort of thing. I never had any plans to nurse in hospital."

"Even when I went out to play on the beach I just had one aim in view: to sit by children. I sat by children because I knew that if I sat long enough the Mothers and Fathers would go to bathe and I would be playing with the children, and incidentally I'd get a sixpence, or a thr'pence. That went in a moneybox at home. They were advertising shoes

from Northampton. And I had an idea: to have a
shoe to slip on my feet with a bow in the front, you
see. "

The photograph shows a smiling teenager among
her friends, with a broad-brimmed hat perched on
her mass of curly hair, and new shoes with bows. It
also shows that Edna was born with weak eye muscles
leading to crossed eyes. Fortunately, as we will see,
someone noticed, and they were to influence her
life, even after surgery corrected the problem, by
directing her attention to nursing and to the hospital ethic — and, to London. So another direction
was opened for her . . . the possibility of nursing in a
hospital.

This possibility came about by chance, an act of
kindness on the part of a virtual stranger.

"When I was in school really my eyes became
bad. When I had to leave to go to Shrewsbury, you
see. That was in the first school, but I have been
told since, that my eyes were wrong ever since I was
a baby. There was an astigmatism in one eye — a
double astigmatism in one eye. The pupil of the eye
was going into the corner. "
"Now we used to have a lady come to stay with
us. She was Lady Kenyon. She came as a visitor in
the house, and she used to take the house, say, for
a month. During that month, various of her chil-
dren would come down. They were all young chil-
dren and they would all go to bathe. But she would
often times sit in the front of our front door. As you
went in through the garden gate there was a little
place in front of the bay window there. There were
a few bricks that made a ledge, and everybody
would sit there sometime or other. Lady Kenyon
wanted to help me. I remember her when I was

quite young, pleading with my Mother to let me go (to hospital). She came to my Mother for years."

"*Well, later on my Mother let me go. I must have been . . . before I was in the County School I went there . . . about 9 I was then. Yes, I was. She pleaded with Mother to let me go to Shrewsbury. Money was so scarce then that the arrangement was made that my Mother took me to the station and put me in the charge of the guard and I was to go all the way to Shrewsbury. You had to change for the train at Machynlleth to go to Shrewsbury. Then going all this journey on my own, we had to wait there until Lady Kenyon would either come herself to the station to meet me or send people up. The first time, Lady Kenyon came there. You'd never believe. We went to the hospital in one of these high cabs. What do you call it? A hansom it was, a hansom. When you sat up there, the horse was in the front and she talked through a hole to the cabby. The cabby was up there behind us. And off we went to the hospital.*"

"*Now I thoroughly enjoyed the ride there, it was a lovely ride. Lady Kenyon was with me, and she handed me over to the nurses and doctors.*"

Then I was frightened. She left, you see. I was frightened to death, at all these extraordinarily clean people all round me. Everybody seemed so prim and so proper. Although I wanted to be a nurse, it wasn't that kind of nurse I wanted to be. I didn't want to be a nurse in a stiff white apron and a stiff hat, and (with) doctors in stiff coats all round you. They seemed . . ."

"*When I had my operation what frightened me more than anything was to see everything white. All the tables white. I was lying back there, and everything white. When I looked back (laughing) there were men with white things all over them. Ooh! It frightened me.*"

*"I had two operations with her, and one after-
wards when I came to London."*

*"When I came out of the theater, I was all
bandaged up, and all the blinds were down in the
wards. You had strict injunctions that you were
not to have any light, you see. I'd been used to
being wild in a way, hadn't I? Because we had the
beach nearby us down in Maesnewydd, if we wanted
to run away we'd only run to the beach didn't we?
We couldn't go anywhere farther; we always came
home when we were hungry. Anyway, to say 'No' to
me, was as good as to say 'I'm going to do it'. Now
I remember quite well going to the window (it was
a big big long window) and pulling the blind up
(at) the corner and seeing the biggest river I'd ever
seen in my life. It was the Severn underneath. It
was beautiful really. (Daft thing to do though,
wasn't it?) But I didn't know. I remember pulling
this bandage up and looking out through that window. It was as clear as anything like that. You
couldn't really see — they made it fixed. Remember
after you've had an operation on your eye, that
your eyes don't focus the same as normal."*

*"I don't remember very much about being into
bed, but I remember my visitor. I remember Lady
Kenyon coming to see me. She didn't bring me any
chocolates or sweets; I didn't even expect them.
Mamma didn't come up because we didn't have
the money. But Lady Kenyon came to see me, and
she brought in her hand a bunch of violets, hot-
house green. I don't know what time of the year it
must have been. I can smell them violets as I never
smelt the wild ones in my life. I also remember
picking up the bandage to have a look at them,
and how big they were. They seemed like . . . these
violets did . . . a huge bunch. She gave me a little
vase to put them in and this vase was by my bedside. I stood and walked around those violets, feeling and feeling round those violets."*

"*Now the time came when I went home. I went home, I was horrified. I had to go home with black glasses. Lady Kenyon took me to the station, put me in the charge of the guard . . . and lo and behold! They were all meeting me there (at the station) and I didn't like these glasses a bit. I wanted to pull them off, and . . . Oh, I had an awful job with those black glasses. They were first shaped so they went (into the corner of the nose); those glasses were sort of beveled. Periodically I had to go to the local doctor where he opened a hole (in the center of the covering), and a larger hole, and a larger hole. And eventually, I got so lazy . . . put it this way: I wanted to read. I used to want to read all the time. The only place I could read in peace, with these black glasses, was (in) the toilet room! I used to go and sit down there and read —OLIVER TWIST, THE THREE MUSKETEERS, and JANE EYRE. I remember reading JANE EYRE there, crying over her very much. I remember reading . . . oh, what's the name . . . wait a minute now . . . by the same author, by Charlotte Bronte. Bronte's books — just imagine the books we had when we were little children!*"*

"*After that, a little later on, I had to go again. I had to be recorrected. Now I went off next time quite bravely, sitting in a carriage. When the time came (to change) at Machynlleth, I got out and the guard told me where I had to go and I went there and arrived at Shrewsbury only to find (that) there was nobody there. I was standing on the station and everybody had gone off. It's a huge station, all covered in. It seemed covered in . . . This was Shrewsbury this time. You never saw such a sight in all your life. It seemed to me terrifically big, this blooming place did. And nobody arriving. I was crying. Out comes one of the porters and asks for whom I was waiting. I said 'I'm waiting for Lady Kenyon'. Just at the moment, a man came running on, in a*

*terrific fix and fuss. It was Lord Kenyon himself
come to take me to the hospital. His wife had died.
He didn't tell me . . . he told the station master,
but I heard."*

*"I went then to the hospital and got it done.
But this was only sort of a correction . . . it wasn't
such a big operation (like the first ones)."*
"But I missed my violets."
"After that the eye operations (were) stopped."

However, Edna had been influenced by this nursing care she had received though it was not yet apparent, and this potential direction in her life remained dormant. In the meantime a far more down-
to-earth role was selected for her . . . she was to become a part time cowherd!

*"During that time, I had left County School
and I was home with my Mother till about 17.
Then I became very discontented. I could see other
people having money. I was home helping my
Mother, at home working hard, and during that
time I did go and help a cousin twice in the
country . . . but I didn't like that really."*
*"My Mother was very generous and this Katy
Felin would come down (for help) to 'Aunty Morgans the Beach', you see. And Aunty Morgans the
Beach would say 'Dear, dear me. Well I'm sure
Ada would like to go up'. My name wasn't Ada at
all, and Ada didn't want to go up to the farm. She
didn't like that woman, at all. It was Swan-neck's
sister this was. (This other elder cousin had an,
elongated neck and was not much liked.) And Ada
(Edna) said 'No, thank you.' 'But you'd like to be
on a farm, wouldn't you?' 'No, I wouldn't.' 'You'd
like to be on a farm for a holiday, wouldn't you?'
'No, I wouldn't', I said. And I kept saying 'I*

wouldn't', but eventually she overpowered me, and off I had to go."

Even today, Welsh farms are very small — a few acres at most especially on those steep grassy hillsides. Most are mixed farming with some arable and some dairy produce, but even when the farm makes its income from sheep or that short hardy wheat and barley, a few cows are always needed for the family. Much of the farm work involves care of livestock — mucking out the byres, and feeding hens, goats and pigs. That together with cleaning house and feeding the farmer and his farm hands, a very parallel activity, is a full time job. There is little leisure time. Edna wasn't at the farm for a holiday.

"I don't even know how I went, but I arrived in 'Y Felin'. . . at a mill, you see. It was a mill and a farm, it was. I worked there for four months. And I worked, and worked . . . I learnt to milk there, and I learnt to call the cows. That is why I have such a strong voice compared to the rest of the family! My Father was wild when he found that I . . ."

Welsh cows are small black animals adept at climbing hillsides. Generally friendly, they will often prance and run apparently for fun, and in running down the hillsides, home to be milked and fed, they could be upsetting to a young town-bred girl.

"She said 'Go for the cows', in Welsh you see. 'Cyrrwch ar ol y buwch, y buwchod.' So off I go, to round them up, you see. Scared stiff of them I was, face forward. And me being so long once, she came at one end of the . . . there was a stream they had to come over, you see, a river that was turning the

47

mill. *She came, and all she did was to . . . 'AA-HOY' she said, 'AA-HOY'. So I thought, 'By Jove, she's doing it' and they all ran towards her. There was I, behind them, with the dog too you see. I was scared stiff of the dogs . . . nasty old snapping things they were. I was scared (laughing) and I was going too far for them. The cows didn't know; they were looking at me, and every time they looked at me I went round them (laughing). So I learnt to call for these cows, and somehow or other they all came in to their special place (in the byre)."*

"*But what annoyed me there — I had to put an old black hat, an old hat hanging up (in the barn) . . . they were very clean really, but I didn't like that hat on my curly hair. Being told my curly hair was nice, I didn't like that hat. I said 'No thank you, I'd rather have the cows skin.' You put a hat on, so that you put your head against the cow, you see. I was milking the cow. Next thing I find some milk coming out and the foot of the cow knocked me over. It was in the bucket, you see. 'Silly old thing. (Laughing) I got up . . . 'Silly old thing, that's not the way to milk a cow'. She said 'Push your head forward, and milk it. Do those two first, those two afterwards . . . '"*

"*You not only press the top (of the teat) and go slowly to the bottom, you press in the proper way. Well, eventually I milked. It was fine leaning your head on the cow watching the milk coming in all frothing up — a lovely feeling really. It was coming higher and higher. You take your bucket and go to the next cow. You couldn't go to ANY cow, you know. That cow would . . . Katy Felin wouldn't let you go to a cow that wouldn't take anybody else only her. Some cows are very choosy. I think I milked three cows that first day."*

"*My cousin was very greedy and she wouldn't let just anybody milk because she had to do the 'tincans'. She usually milked every cow, and after they'd all been milked she went right round them again and got the last milk. The last milk is the 'tincans' . . . the last milking is the richest, or supposed to be, you see. So I learnt to milk the cows."*

"Listen now . . . I also helped with the potatoes, with the feeding of these farmers. I was four months there. At the end of the four months, knowing I could ride, she actually gave me the loan of her bike. I was to go and see my Mother. She gave me ten shillings for four months. I thought then it was too little. She never gave me any money at all during that time. I was two miles from home and I was going to have a ride on the bike. Well, I thought 'That's fine', but on the handlebars of this bike were pounds and pounds of butter. (I'd learnt to make butter too. All made into round pounds with a cow stamped on it and everything, you know.) And on the back was another big basket of butter. Now I was to take them to the shop in Towyn and to bring back sugar and tea. That was the only thing they bought. Then I could ride home to see my Mother, while they were exchanging the baskets."

"Now off I go to see my Mother. I said, 'Look what she's given me' and I held up the ten shillings. 'Is that all?' 'Look'. And my Mam said, 'Well, I never. Isn't it nice of her giving you that.' . . ."

Ten shillings in those days was worth, on face value, two dollars, which represented less than 2 cents a week: hardly a career direction! Fortunately, Edna was already independent enough to look out for herself and to take those opportunities that presented themselves. Seeing that her brothers and sisters had been liberated by the cities of England: London and Liverpool perhaps that was where her next direction lay?

Chapter 3

Role Conflicts

'*When I first left Towyn, what I did was to go to Liverpool for a holiday with my Mother to see my Father. He was working in Liverpool, just for a short time. While we were there I said to my Mother 'I'm not coming home, you know. I am going to the children's hospital in Liverpool to work.'*'

'*It was THE Liverpool Children's Hospital. I was determined to go to nurse. Now, as I was away I was determined not to go back. My Mother was rather despondent about it, but still I said 'I'm going'. Now, of all the awful things then, they refused to accept me, to nurse children because I had my glasses.*'

'*I was under the age for general training. I was 17 then, just 17. 'I'm still not coming home'. Then I applied to somewhere up the London Road*' in Liverpool. I applied to the Mill Road Infirmary. I was immediately asked to go for an interview. So I went in there and they must have thought I was a bonny looking girl. I never said a lie about my age but they did say at the time 'You are quite mature for your age, and you're very keen on trying'. So they accepted me to try my general nursing, which then took four years, now it only takes three. Because it was a poor law (hospital), they were paying me a little bit . . . I forget how little it was . . . instead of me paying them. I didn't have to pay a fee to go for my training, but I had to work an extra year, you see. So I was accepted there and Mamma and Dadda went home."

"I think I must have gone home with my Mother and then come back . . . I arrived in Liverpool and my cousin from Bootle met me. When I got back into the hospital it was seven o'clock in the evening. The gateman said 'You go to such and such a place', and I went to such and such a place. I was sent up into the ward. I happened to go on the men's ward. This was a bronchial . . . a chesty ward you see. Everybody was coughing. Now the senior nurses used to go down for their meals first and they used to leave some staff on the ward, and then we would go down afterwards, you see. So there were no senior nurses there. Well it so happened, as I was a probationer, the junior nurse, in the ward, I was told . . . blissfully like this (laughing) to go round and collect all these sputum mugs. I didn't know anything about them. Well a patient told me what to do. Carry a tray and carry all these 36 sputum mugs. I was to wash them. Oooh! You know I didn't know then that we had a thing whereby you could put them in like a flush, and you could press a pedal and clean them. I started washing them under the tap, like I would have washed dishes. Oooh! I nearly said that night, 'I don't want to be a nurse'."

"But anyway, I overcame that . . . knowing

51

there were patients there that I could ask. There were patients that were part of the hospital, perhaps that had been there many years, you see. They knew more about the ward than we did. Since it was poor law, there was always one or two around helping the young nurses. We'd say (in whispers) 'What have I got to do?' Anyway, now I was in that ward. Oh, I was ever so pleased."

"I was in my glory, I really was. When we were nursing in there I was very very happy really. I happened to land there with a Sister Handley. This was just at the end of the war, 1918. The only worry there that I had . . . all these wards were one on top of another: 1B, 2B, 3B, 4 and all the rest of it. To me that was all new, but I quite enjoyed being with the other girls."

"You had to be very smartly dressed. You had fifteen clean aprons given to you. That meant one for every day and one for an emergency . . . about seven frocks. They provided them in this poor law place, you see . . . and hats which were just pieces of material as far as I was concerned. You had to twist them so that they stayed on your head . . . you just put two pins either side and they became like an envelope on your head. Oh, I thought I was IT. And a high collar on your neck, you see. I was as happy as Punch. We were all held up straight, there was no question of it . . . we were all held up like that . . . and cuffs on our arms, you know."

"What amused me really was the first month's pay! . . . I was in the back of the (pay) queue, you see . . . my first month's pay was due. I was as pleased as Punch. (Laughing) I was in the back of the queue and I was told by my neighbour that, very very shortly, before the next payday, there would be another nurse behind me, so I was moving up. Seeing all these senior nurses: these ward-nurses, these sisters, all ahead and they all looked so smart. I could see a matron, with lace round her neck. I

*said to the girl next to me 'Never mind, there is a
chance to get up even further than one of those' –
looking at the sisters. 'There is a chance to get lace
round your neck'."*

Having now taken a direction leading to hospital
nursing, it wasn't Iong before Edna's ambition, to
get ahead, asserted itself, even though it was ex-
pressed in a joke. She wanted to do well at nursing,
well enough eventually to wear lace at her throat as
a matron, the highest point at which she could aspire in those days.

*"Then I saw the screen put up. My senior nurse
on the ward happened to be a nurse who had been
nursing mental patients, and she was really funny,
you know. I said 'What's behind the screen?' She
said 'Go and have a look.' So I went behind the
screen and saw a covered bed. I saw this covered
bed rise up and flop down and it rose up again
and flopped down, and I ran to this nurse. I was
terrified. I said 'You know, you've made a mistake.
It's alive.' She didn't even tell me it was a dead
person. 'You've made a mistake. Yes, you have. I
know it's moved.' So she took me behind the screen
and told me what that was. Although they had died,
they were not really dead . . . the body hadn't died.
But I was a bit nervous about going behind a screen,
after that, I can tell you. (Laughing) It's a weird
thing first, you know. Terribly weird."*

*"Well now, they were all off the ward. All the
nurses were evidently at a lecture. There was only
the Sister Handley, whom I loved . . . (She was lovely,
she was one of the gentle sisters) . . . and myself. There
was an emergency case. Liverpool is on the docks,
and an emergency case arrived from the docks. There
was a lot of pneumonia in this ward . . . in our
spare time we used to make pneumonia jackets,*

chest jackets, all of cotton wool. They had cotton wool padding them, and we'd have tapes at the back, so they would keep on the patients, to keep them warm . . . yes, you had to do it, you know. Now Sister Handley said that there was a patient brought in and I was to help her. I was ever so pleased. I was with the senior person on the ward. She was so gentle . . . now you do this way . . . you do that way . . . and I thought 'I'm happy to be a nurse'. I was as happy as the day was long. Nothing was too much."

"And she said 'You know, . . . ('little nurse' she called me) . . . You know, little nurse,' she said, 'I have never had a new patient die.' So I was ever so pleased. I was one of them. Nobody died on this ward. But I had in my mind this other person behind the screen, you see. It couldn't have been pneumonia. And it wasn't really; it was . . . you would call it a form of cancer today. Anyway, I forget the name even. But anyway, a telephone message came and she had to go down. She was behind a screen, and I was doing little things in the ward. She said 'Now, little nurse, I want you to stay while I'm away, and see that this patient doesn't get out of bed.' He was a sailor, you see. He'd been brought in from the docks. She said 'Now remember, I never lose a pneumonia patient, but we have to be very careful. See that he doesn't get out of bed.' Well, of course, he was in a sort of delirium and they didn't have these tranquilizers to quiet them down. Not as much then as you can now. The man was in high temperature. He hadn't been in the casualty ward; he was an emergency patient. So I, dutifully . . . when he started being hot and bothered, when he was delirious . . . I was fighting, fighting hard, and he was a big man, you see. He was lovely looking. He had a beard on. Oh, he was lovely looking. I thought he was like Jesus, you see. You know, I was watching him and he was fighting. The only way I could do *anything was to lie on him, so I lay on him, with my arm over, and that's how (I was when) Sister came back."*

"Now, she said 'That's very good of you but never do that anymore. Just tighten the bedclothes, and you'll keep him in. It's already made for it.' So I thought, 'Well never mind, I held him in.' Mind you, it was hard work."

"We were two in a bedroom. There was very little in it, but it did have a dressing-table-cum-chest-of-drawers; all in one with a little looking glass on one side, you know. We had to be very tidy, and we were told that we had to keep that corner of the room, where we were, tidy."

"Junior nurses went off the ward at night . . . and we went for our suppers. A senior nurse would sit at the end of the table, and as a junior nurse came (in) so you would (move) around the table. So you knew very well, just by looking at the table, the person right opposite you would be a senior nurse, or she'd be on the next table. Anyway, I was sitting there, and, I just couldn't eat. Oh, I wanted a drink. Oh, I wanted a drink, I did. I wanted a drink more than anything. Sitting at that table, I didn't want that food at all. I was right off it, worse than usual. But anyway, after we'd finished our meal we were free, and this was about eight o'clock. I had been given by one of the nurses a gift of a little flowerpot — roughly speaking about two inches high. I had nothing else in my bedroom then."

"Well, I was running down the corridor to the bathroom to get a drink of water out of this little flower pot. It was pink . . . I can remember that . . . and I drank, and drank, and drank, and drank, and drank. I remember undressing myself, and folding my clothes on the side of my bed. I don't remember a thing more, until I found myself now in a ward. It was now me that was delirious.

I had caught diphtheria from that sailor. Evidently, even though he was brought in a chest ward he hadn't been diagnosed before he came up. So I caught diphtheria. Anyway, I didn't know."

"Just a day or two previous to this, my senior nurse, who was a practical joker, walked me through a mental ward. She had been a mental nurse in Withington Main, before she'd come to Mill Road."

Since the Mill Road Infirmary was a poor law institution, it was bound to care in a general way for all who could not afford (to pay): the indigent, the lost and the strayed. Thus the hospital had wards devoted even to long-term sickness, for in many cases there was nowhere else for the patient to go except perhaps a workhouse. The mental wards was usually full of the feeble minded and old, deserted as difficult and troublesome by their families. Today they would be put discretely into nursing homes, but for those who could afford nothing at the beginning of the century, the mental ward of a poor law hospital was all to which they could look forward.

"She said to me before I went in there. 'When I take you through this ward, don't look at them. Just walk through and don't look at any bed.' So I walked dutifully straight through but out of the corner of my eye . . . do you know, I nearly ran. Oh, everybody seemed to be getting out of his bed to look at me and run after me. I was scared. Now when I had diphtheria, you see, when I was in the ward, that stuck in my mind. Do you see? And I don't know whether it was the rise in my temperature, but I was screaming like anything. I remember quite well. The person who was acting host sister, looking after me now: a fever patient. She was as hard as anything. She now had the job of

keeping me to lie down. She was pressing me down and making me lie. Suddenly out of all this turmoil, this fear in this ward, and I suppose the high temperature I had developed, Sister Handley appeared like an angel through it. She just sat by my side and I was quiet in no time. Whether they may have given me an injection, I don't know."

"But after that, I was sent to a fever hospital. I had to be under observation first (in my own hospital). As soon as they found I was diphtheric I was sent to a proper fever hospital. 'Forsackly' it was. Then I was there for a month. That was Christmas."

"When I came back, apparently cured, I came back to the hospital, only to be told I had to go home for a month's holiday. Sister Handley came to me quietly at the time and she said 'Now, little nurse, you've been very ill' It had been touch and go for me to have a tracheotomy. 'Well', she said 'You've been very ill. If you're not better in a month, take two months, and if you're not better in two months, take three months'."

"My brother Willie came up to Liverpool to bring me home. When I arrived home, my brother evidently went back to school, and I found my Father in bed. So being used to nursing a bit on the men's wards, and he a man, I dutifully nursed him. I don't think even my parents knew how ill I had been, really. It seemed to me that I worked so hard at home, I was jolly glad to get back to Liverpool at the end of the month. I didn't realise that I was as ill as I still was."

Unfortunately Edna's ambition was stronger than she was, and she returned to the Mill Road Infirmary too soon. She had not yet really recovered.

"Well, after returning I was on the ward for

57

*about two days and my hands got stiff, and my feet
got stiff. I found I couldn't even move my fingers.
Sister Handley saw me and she watched. Then I
got throat paralysis. I was taken to another bed,
sobbing my heart out. Absolutely broken hearted I
was, not so much with not being able to move my
feet, and hands, but that I wasn't going to the
payday, you see. I wanted to be second from the
end, sort of thing . . . I was broken hearted. The
old major came. He was the medical superintendent. He came in with the matron, and there they
were, both trying to tell me that they had really
made a mistake and taken me one year too soon. If
I went home and had twelve months holiday, they
would be more than willing to take me back at the
end of twelve months. It broke my heart."*

*"Anyway, I went home and I stayed home for
a time. I was very very discontented. Now I could
see all the other people moving up in that pay
queue. That was in my mind. During that time in
Liverpool they had set an examination and I passed
it. I was very good on writing notes. You got these
lectures with the Sister Tutor, and I was very good
at writing and abbreviating notes, you see. I had
been complimented on this even in my geography
lessons: in not taking the full lesson but just writing notes on it. (Now it was for nothing.) I was
upset. Oh, I was upset."*

*"During that whole twelve months, I was get-
ting on for 18. Willie was getting on for 16 and
getting all the laurels in school. Willie could do
everything and Ada couldn't do anything. That
sort of feeling came. I thought, I'm going back to
nursing, I'm going back to nursing, and when I
go back to nursing I won't even tell them when I'm
ill. But you get that inferiority complex. It's terrible. Children, you know, brothers and sisters could
really and truly be cruel to each other. 'You weren't
ill, you couldn't do it . . . ' When I came home I*

was apparently better, and you know what I'm like. I just go until I drop? But anyway, Mamma all this time must have known. It seems that they must have had a letter. I did see this letter from the doctor in the fever ward. It had gone to the medical superintendent of the hospital and he'd said that I had a very bad throat. Now, that's the worst thing against you, when you're nursing. Because of the dry heat . . . the dry heat and the wooden floors, upset you . . . but it hadn't upset me until I caught this diphtheria. I'd never had my tonsils out and of course that wasn't helpful either."

But this episode was over. Edna had tried a nursing career, had tried being independent of the family, and had tried to show that she too could succeed. She had apparently failed and she was back to 'square one' — back to manual labor. Prospects were not at all bright for her.

Chapter 4:

Backward Steps
– In Service

'*Well anyway, eventually I was home and now taking a great interest in everything being scrupulously clean. When my sisters came home, they always wanted to go as far as Barmouth. I would turn my Mother's room upside down and solidly went around cleaning and cleaning, and always cooked a meal for them when they came home at six o'clock.*'

"*All this was hard work there in a way, because my Mother was also very clean, you see. It was nothing for Mother to tell you, when you'd cleaned a bedroom . . . we didn't polish so much then, we sort of washed it with soap and water . . . and soap put on a fairly dry cloth . . . we would have to go UNDER the lino too. What we'd*"

do, we'd turn up the lino and go up all the edges.
Now it was all hard work when you are turning a
big huge bed. I didn't really realise that I was tax-
ing my own strength. The doctor had said that I
had worked too hard, too young. Now all this was
against me . . . even working with Katy 'Felin', at
the Felin farm, because I would get up six o'clock
in the morning there and be out in the fields pretty
early. Mind you I was supposed to go to bed at six
o'clock too. But the sun was shining, so you didn't
go to bed at six o'clock if there was a window you
could slide out of. Only you just jumped out of it
and played the rest of the time in the field, and
went back the same way."

Edna was never sickly; she was a strong healthy
young girl. However the servant's life is never easy,
and coupled with young impatience to get on rather
than endurance, the life could be destructively hard,
both to health and happiness. So when prospects
appeared to give no hope of anything better, Edna
had difficulty in accepting her servant's role. However before the inevitable rebellion, there were dis-
tractions.

"The time while I was home from 14 to nearly
19 (except for the year or so in Liverpool) wasn't
unhappy, in a way . . . No, I can't say it was un-
happy, it was only unhappy in the last few months,
or rather the year or two."
"The end of the war came, 1918 sort of thing,
and the boys were returning from the war. I was
going down to the beach one day, and somebody
said behind me 'I've carried you on my shoulder.' I
said', 'I beg your pardon?' I was with other girls,
you see. 'I've carried you on my shoulder before
today'. I said, 'You never have.' I was as tall as
the man who was speaking to me. He turned out to

61

be a boy called Gwilym Arthur . . . he was Sophie's age."

"I got to know him really this way. There were visitors from Ynys Maengwyn staying in our house, and they had a black Nanna. The husband was a soldier and he was returning here, and the wife and the little daughter child and the black Nanna were staying in our house. They took the whole house for the summer. There's a 'let' for you! And they had all their meals in Ynys Maengwyn. Well, because they wanted the little girl to speak English . . . she was only a baby . . . as well as their own language (Welsh); they used to take me in a motor car to Ynys Maengwyn. Well, when they couldn't get the chauffeur from Ynys Maengwyn, to come down . . . they hired a car from a garage. Gwilym Arthur was the man who was driving. After the war he was working in this garage. By this time I was sitting in the front seat with the driver, I was. The other portion (of the car) was closed in, you see. The Nanna was holding the baby. I wanted to hold the baby, but anyway, Nanna was holding the baby and . . . I forget her name . . . the lady was there. All of a sudden, Gwilym Arthur said 'Funny how we're put together isn't it?' and he was just laughing and we went off to Ynys Maengwyn. But by this time, I went into Ynys Maengwyn. Now the car . . . there was no question of him coming back for us . . . he was like a taxi . . . now we had the car from Ynys Maengwyn, the Corbett Hotel. They were the lords of the land, you see. I think the lady was a niece, just the niece."

Mostly, the young people of that day and age met through the church or chapel, and their socials (dances and picnics.) The chapel summer picnic was a highlight of the year, when the entire congregation, even those that hadn't been to a service for months would turn out for the day's fun. Sometimes it involved a charabanc ride to a resort town or, since Towyn was a resort already, a ride up into the mountains for a picnic on a hillside. On one occasion everyone was treated to a wild ride down a mountain side sitting in straw-lined wagons from the slate quarries . . . the Welsh equivalent of an American hayride. Even on a religious outing there were opportunities for young people to pair off and disappear for a few frantic minutes.

Besides . . . Gwilym Arthur wasn't the only young man on the beach.

"Anyway, I took the child round the grounds and in taking him round the grounds, we wandered into a garden. The gardener of this place was a man called Mr. Strawn, an Englishman. He had two children and the boy, Gordon Strawn, was also in my class, but he was shy. He was an English boy, you see. Now, he and I went round playing with this baby, round the gooseberry bushes. We had a good time with this baby (laughing) only to find now that we were reprimanded most severely by the black Nanna for letting this child run wild with us, you see. Well, eventually I was sent back in disgrace, not by the mistress but by the black Nanna."

"Well, I used to go up and do this many many at time. I'd tell Gordon Strawn when to expect us and we used to have a run round the garden with this baby. (The child was) just running age, just starting to run. We had a good time with this little thing."

"Funny about Gordon Strawn again, you see. His family lived in a lodge at Ynys Maengwyn, but after his Father died they came to live down on the beach at Towyn, which was near where we lived. When his Father died his Mother had to keep visitors, so there was only one place for them to go . . . down by the beach."

"While his Mother was letting visitors and we were letting visitors, remember when we let to visitors we let the WHOLE house and our beds were downstairs. And if we couldn't get in downstairs, then down in the field. There was a double bed for Mamma and Dadda in the back parlour, and there were two double beds in the back kitchen. The rest of us had to sleep in a shed that my Father made, or in a tent. We had a bell tent. We were camping; we didn't mind how soon we were shoved out. But if we were unlucky enough not to be able to go in one of those beds, we just waited until the visitors went to bed and saw the lights going out, and then we ran home to lie on the couch. That's how we slept and we worked hard all day."

"One of these times when I went down to the beach, I was sitting on the beach watching lights in Maesnewydd and Gordon Strawn walks from his house and he said 'Oh, are you in the same pickle, too? I'm waiting for that big couch in that room.' 'And I'm waiting for the couch in my room.' We literally had to sleep like that. Well, by this time (we were) 18 or 19. We didn't mind, we were quite happy. It was only for a summer. We used to watch these sunsets. Well anyway we were very happy."

"Until Sophie came home . . . it was discord as soon as Sophie came in. She seemed to set sparks to everything. I really did leave home and I was glad to get away."

Sophia Morgans was the 4th of the family of ten, seven years older than Edna and five years older than Maria. She was an adult and felt that she had the right to be obeyed by her young sisters. Later in life she was to join the 'Jehova's Witnesses', the 'Brethren' and show all signs of extreme religious mania. Even at this time she was 'too good to be true'. That didn't help her relationship with spirited siblings. Besides Sophie there were two other older sisters, Margaretta, thirteen years older than Edna, and Jane Mary, nine years older. They were all established in careers and they were more elder relatives rather than sisters.

"Anyway, later, my sisters came home and during that time Sophie and Willie had gone out to pick blackberries. They came home and I was just finishing the kitchen floor and I was coming to the door. Mamma being so particular, not only about washing the floor, but drying it too . . . it was red and blue tiles, sort of a dark blue; they were . . . many a time we had to wash the floor in buttermilk and water. It sort of gave a sheen on it, but so little you couldn't see it. Anyway, I was at the very end."

"Sophie came in and she said she wanted to go somewhere, and I said 'But look, there's one (toilet) outside the door there.' I was on my knees in the doorway and there was a toilet just outside the door. She didn't go. She meant to push past me to go upstairs, and I said 'You can't go in, you see, I've just washed the floor'. As she pushed past me, I pushed her and she put her foot in the bucket, and SCREAMED! Now, when you hear a scream, when you're busy working, . . . well, I pushed her further in. What I did was to push her further down, my bucket slopped all over the floor. And I had been scrubbing hard in order to finish. I got up. The scream must have upset Willie too, for he came and clouted me. Now it frightened me to see what I had done. I got up, and I ran."

"I ran and I ran and I ran. You can believe it or not, I ran through the fields, onto the (railway) line and I ran on the line (knowing where to run mind you — on the side of the line) until I landed

*in Barmouth, 12 miles away. I threw my apron
away. That shows what fear can do to anybody. I
was not quite 19."*

*"That was a Saturday, and we always aimed
at a twelve o'clock dinner. Mamma was cooking
actually, with chops on the fire for Dadda. Dadda
came home on Saturday, since it was a special day.
We used to have chops and a very good dinner on
Saturday, and we all had to work like blazes for it,
'cause we knew the boys were coming in to go out
and play football. My job was to wash dishes all
the time. It was pretty grim really when you come
and look back at it. When these girls came home
they didn't work. You see, no, I had to wash dishes.
'No, no, it had to be done now'."*

Such were prospects, and the reasons for her
rebellion. The incident with Sophie was a last straw.
However Edna's circumstances were no different
from those of thousands of young girls in thousands
of households across Britain at that time. Families
were large, elder siblings were adults compared to
the younger, and the youngest girl was expected to
help her Mother at home. They were virtual servants
to their own brothers and sisters. Brothers however
didn't fare so badly. Notice that it was Willie, two years
younger than Edna who was invited out to collect
blackberries while Edna scrubbed floor, and it was to
get the boys out to their football game that she would
end up by washing dishes . . . for ten! If the recipi-
ent of such treatment had any initiative, something
was bound to happen.

*"I went to my Uncle John's in Barmouth and
told him 'I've run away from home, you know.' I'd
cooled down by this. 'I've run away from home,
you know.' So, he said 'How did you come?' I said*

'I've run.' I ran, ran, ran, ran . . . (whispers). See, when I was frightened too, my nose used to bleed, terribly, (so I was a mess when I had arrived.) He kept me there that night and let me sleep, in his bedroom, really. He was about 67 then and alone, his wife had died, and his son had gone away. The next day was Sunday . . . I hadn't got clothes you know. I was as I was, in working clothes."

"Uncle John gave me half-a-crown, which was the price of going home by train. Now he said 'You'll go?' I said 'Yes.' I had in my mind that I knew how to walk to Fairbourne, but this time I didn't go on the railway line because he had told me that I might have been run down, or anything might have happened."

"I walked along the road. I walked right round on the coastal road and I landed in Fairbourne. I went now to a shop, and in some of these shops you find notices of jobs. I saw a job in Fairbourne for a public house. I was scared stiff of going into a public house but I saw a job for a housemaid. Well, I thought I knew how to make beds and didn't think about me being in a public house. I went into a huge hotel; it seemed to me. Everything was massive. I said 'I've come to apply for the job.' I must have looked small for a person really. Mind you I'd washed and cleaned, and tidied myself as well as I could. September it was, so perhaps I wasn't as bad as I think I was. So she said 'When can you come?' 'Tomorrow.' 'Have you got a black frock?' 'Yes.' 'Have you got a white apron?' 'Yes.'"

"I hadn't got any such thing. So I went to Fairbourne Station and out of the half-a-crown I paid my fare to Towyn, but I got off just before the station, or, the stop before Rhyd yr Onen. Tonfanai it was. Got off at Tonfanai. I knew it was as easy for me to walk from Tonfanai as it was to go to the station and feel all, sort of Sunday-morning-ish. I

67

*could easy go home that way — across the fields.
Off I went."*

"When I arrived home . . . we had a sort of
private lane to go down home . . . and there I saw
my Mother. It was the most heart breaking of all –
I saw my Mother take her apron off, and just say
'Ada Bach' (little Edna) and just put her face on
my shoulder (tearfully). I flew upstairs."

"Mind you a minute. I was coming home in a
terribly bad temper, really. I was going to go. I
didn't know where a black frock was, but I knew a
white apron, belonged to Sophie, (originally she'd
been nursing too). Well anyway, I went upstairs.
Maria had a black frock for dancing. Somebody
else's castdown, you know. I looked at this frock,
tried it on. I went upstairs, ran past my Mother. I
went upstairs, and I banged the door – in temper
really – because I didn't want to cry. I banged the
door and I went and looked at this frock which
belonged to Maria. I went under the bed for an old
wicker basket where Sophie had kept her nursing
aprons. They were very long. You can just imagine nursing aprons, with a big bib on them. They
weren't the ones I was wanting at all. They were
miles too big for me up here. I thought if I cut the
top of them, they'd look like my Mother's. In my
mind, I put one apron on. One apron, not two or
three. I could have put two or three, but I only put
one, and this one black frock."

"The frock on me, when I looked in the
mirror . . . In order to have a mirror, we had to
take one of these mirrors from the watch-em-a-call-
it and stand down and turn round in it. Turn
round in front of it and then we saw the length of
our frock. Well, while I was doing that and feeling
'I'm not going to cry, I'm not going to cry, I'm not
going to cry'. . . in comes my Father."

"My Father was very quiet and very clever really. They must have sent for him, on a Monday.

He just sat on the bed and said 'Hello'. 'Hello.
(Quietly) What you doing?' 'I'm getting a black
frock', I told him. 'What are you going to do?' 'I'm
going to work, as a waitress. I'm going to be a
housemaid, a housemaid in Fairbourne.' 'You know
very well,' he said, 'in that place, it's a public
house . . . it's a plain public house. You know very
well that you can't stand them. You don't like
drunken people.' 'No, I don't, but I'll have nothing to do with the drunken people, I'm going to
make beds . . . it is only a housemaid.' I didn't
look once at my Father."

"Now, it so happened that when I had this
frock in my hand, I had to turn round and I saw
my Father. I just flew into his arms. (Crying and
searching for a handkerchief.)"

"My Mother . . . evidently she had been phoning to Llew, and Llew (in London) had sent a
wire back 'Send her up here for a holiday.' Sophie
was in Blythe Road (London) then, and they per-
suaded me that it would be much better to go for a
holiday and to go back to London with Sophie. I
said 'Not likely'."

South Wales is fairly industrial, based principally
on its coal mining, and apart from the periodic
slumps and industrial unrest it can offer jobs for the
population. However, rural Wales had, and still has,
very few jobs for its youth, and it has always suffered
by having its best young people leave for opportunities in England, principally in the larger cities,
Liverpool, Manchester and London. This applied to
quiet coastal towns like Towyn as well, but since Edna's
Mother was from Liverpool, the choice for the Morgans was the port of Liverpool or the capital London. At this time, Margaretta, Llewellyn, Jane Mary,
and Sophie were all working in London.

"We were all in London. Everybody in our place; they only had one aim, either to Liverpool or to London. I wasn't going back to a job, I was going for a holiday, and I was going for a holiday to my elder brother, really you see. I had very few days in which to get ready. During those few days . . ."

"I had, during my time in Towyn, saved up through helping to look after children on the beach and this bathing van stunt. I used to help on the farm at the beach where they kept the tents and bathing vans. There weren't many farm labourers but there were two bachelor brothers and one maiden sister, a spinster maid, that's all there were. They were our milkmen too. It wasn't so much of a big farm, (but they did have the summertime bathing van business). I used to be in the little shop. And brushing out the vans . . . remember they were full of sand . . . the one(s) on wheels. It was a lovely job that was but I had no money for it, you know. No, no money at all. We just wanted to help, and the only payment I ever had for that, was that I used to go to the farmhouse for dinner. I remember going back to the farm for dinner after being hot on the beach (hiring out these bathing costumes), to a rice pudding that had been in the oven all morning. BIG big ones, they seemed much bigger than any dish we'd got. There wasn't just one . . ."

"The way I had money was this: when we hired these bathing costumes out . . . The bathing costumes were like coarse sacking, and when you put it on you it really scratched, and it sort of got you ready for going in the water. There were skirts on the women's bathing costumes and they came down below the knee in a frill. That was elastic and so that scratched to begin with, and you were lucky to get one to fit you. That frill on your knee might come down to your ankle, you see. You just looked like that at it . . . 'Will that one do?' you'd say. They'd say 'Yes'. Then some-

times you'd have them come back and say 'It won't even go on me'. Some of them were so small. You had a hat on your head, a cap. You never went in without a cap . . . not a rubber cap, but one of these coarse old caps on your head that had a frill, again on elastic. You dutifully tucked every bit of hair in underneath, you know. It didn't stop it from getting wet. No, not a bit, but we thought it did, you see. (Laughing) The salt didn't go on our hair, we were sure it didn't. Half of them never went as far as dipping their heads in water. (Laughing)"

"Now, if your bathing van went down to the water you had a chance of letting out some shoes too. You'd find a few stones in front of you and one would shout to another, 'Will you go and get me some shoes?' These shoes were corded, like straw things, and there was so much tape put on some of these that you were a long time putting them around your leg, you see. They went down and around, all crisscross around your leg, and they came up to the frill. So you were truly fastened up. Perhaps four girls would go in one (van). Honestly, when you opened the door and you'd look at each other . . . (laughing)."

"When the English people, the visitors, came around, suppose something came to about tenpence, then they would let me have a shilling. I kept the twopence of that, you see. I remember working ever so hard on that. During the two or three years I used to do that, I actually got 8 War Savings (Bonds) at ten shillings each, by that. So it was only four pounds, wasn't it? But they were War Savings."

Until 1978 Britain used a system of currency in which:

4 farthings = 1 penny
2 halfpennies = 1 penny
12 pennies = 1 shilling

20 shillings = 1 pound
21 shillings = 1 guinea

Thus it took Edna 500 two-penny tips to make her four pounds. The four pounds would have been worth about $16 then.

"So going back now to the time when I was leaving home . . . going for a holiday to London. I began in my mind to plan. 'If I get to London, you'll never get me back'. So I sold those 8 War Savings to my Mother for five pounds. She gave me five pounds. I didn't pay for the fare, and the five pounds was mine. I'd never held five pounds in my hand before. I had finally given in because in going to London now, even though Sophie was the person (with me)."

"We traveled all night, and all that night I was preached to, and preached to and preached to. I was looking forward to London, really. In my mind, London was going to be a beautiful place. Sophie was seven years older than me, and Sophie had always been ill. When she was born, you know, the doctor said to my Mother (that) she would be better dead. She was born with a bad heart, in a way, AND she had a temper. Well anyway, this night she preached, and preached, and preached. The main theme of this sermon was 'Put a Price on yourself'. Well, I was far more keen to go to sleep, than to put a price on myself. In fact, I didn't even understand what she meant. I never listened to Sophie, because she was always preaching, you see. She was saying 'Put a Price on yourself' all the time, and that's all I remember as I fell asleep . . ."

Chapter 5

London

'*Well, I arrived in London. I was ever so disappointed. We had to walk from the station right down to Holland Park, and it was early early in the morning. We had to walk from Paddington Station to Holland Park (some miles) and all I saw were the same stars and the same sky as in Wales . . . and the dirtiest places I ever saw in my life. I began to hate London then.*"

"*We went to stay in Holland Park. Gretta was staying in Holland Park, and Sophie. Gretta was working in the Shipping Office. Sophie was working in Blythe Road. Sophie was also going in for music; she was going under Evangeline Florence for voice in her spare time. Jane Mary was up there too at the time. She was actually teaching then in Norfolk, Jane Mary was. She'd come up there for a* holiday and we all met there. Llew was living in Baker Street."

"Gretta and Sophie went to work everyday. Jane Mary was taking me about, and she gave me such a royal time, she did honestly. But I had five pounds in my pocket, John. Every time we went on buses I said 'I'll pay'. When I went with my brother (Llew), my brother said 'No, you want to keep it'. 'No,' I said, 'I'll pay'. Now, I was very generous and very independent, and they let me pay. Now there came an end to that five pounds — didn't there? During that first week in London, that I was there with Jane Mary, we saw Chu-chin Chow, Maid of the Mountains, and we saw The Merchant of Venice, and we went round the shops. We had trips on buses. Wherever I could, I paid. That was an end to the five pounds in a week. Especially when I was paying for them too, you see."

"I said to Llew when I was nearly finished . . . I said to Llew. 'Look Llew, I'm not going home. I'm not going home to work anymore. Other people are earning and I'm going to earn'. 'Well, what can you do?' 'I'm going nursing'. My Mother had instilled into me that it would be far better in service, but I said 'I'm not going into service, I'm going nursing'."

"So the first job I had was in Croydon, looking after a little boy of two to three years of age. His Father and Mother had come from Africa, and he had two older sisters. I answered an advert, or rather Llew answered, after Llew and I looked up a paper, and I said 'That's the one'. A boy of two, that's what I wanted."

"So off I went to this new job. In West Norwood it was first. I saw Crystal Palace . . . we stayed, mind you, in Crystal Palace. It was like a holiday, you now. We were in digs for the first week, you see. All I had to do was walk this boy, dress him *and put him back to bed. This boy of two wasn't trained very well. He was out to see too. He'd come back to London too from Africa. He never went to sleep so it was really a hard day. All I was doing was walking behind this boy, wherever he led. We all walked behind him. But anyway, I thought I was in heaven. Like in a hotel it was, you see."*

"The following week their furniture had come and now we went to a new house near Croydon . . . one of these big houses. A beautiful house it was. We were settling into the house. They had engaged a cook, they'd engaged a housemaid, they'd engaged a man servant for the garden, and all were there."

"Then about three days after we'd arrived there, I got up in the morning to find the cook drunk, and the gardener fast asleep in the kitchen. She (the cook) was dead drunk. We couldn't waken her up. They were literally expelled straight away. I said 'I'll make a fire for you'. You see how silly it is to go (and volunteer). 'I'll make a fire for you'. 'Well, I can cook bacon, on a fire'. So I eventually landed with the cook's job, plus looking after the boy. There was a housemaid there but she didn't offer to do anything. So then, I was landed with this job: cook. Mrs. Efgrave came down and helped me with cooking too later on, when we had to get an evening meal."

"Now before the end of this month came we found that the housemaid had skidaddled, stealing a lot of stuff. So now I was a housemaid plus . . . General factotum I was in that house."

"The end of the month came and Mrs. Efgrave was very nice to me. She tried a coat on me. Then she said 'Do you like it?' 'Yes, very nice'. It was a very smart coat, absolutely tailored, and it absolutely fitted me. So she said 'Would you like that instead of your month's pay?' So I said, 'No, thank

75

*you'. I had no money at all in my pocket. So I said
'No, thank you'. She didn't pay me that day."*

*"Well, during that day, we were moving a bed.
It was one of these iron bedsteads, you see. She was
moving that side and I happened to be on this
side. She was moving that towards me and I was
pulling and I pulled the top rail off it. She said
'Well, you'll have to go and get it mended'. So I
dutifully took it, holding the boy, and I dutifully
took it to a place to get it mended. Then she said
'We'll pay you your month's wages, when we get
the bill for that.' When the bill came back, the next
day, she said 'Now I'll deduct the money from your
month's money'. It was MORE than my
money . . . more than my month's wages, which was
very little. So I managed to get a little bit of my
money for the next month, and I flew to Llew in
Baker Street, and told him what had happened.
He said 'Now look here. You go back and take this
letter to your mistress.' It said that I had not signed
a form whereby I paid for breakages and that I was
not moving this bed on my own. I didn't have to
show it to her, I had to show it to Mr. Efgrave. I
showed it to Mr. Efgrave and as I showed it to Mr.
Efgrave, he turned to his wife and said, 'You pay
it at once'. She paid me my money, and I clung to
this money like blazes."*

Money from earnings represented a good measure of independence. Being in service, it represented almost the only measure, since all other
things, the clothes she wore, the times she kept, the
food she ate, even the people she associated with,
were under the control of her master or mistress.
Edna had no grand vision of the liberation of the
working classes or the liberation of woman, she was
thinking only of the liberation of 'Edna.' To start with
she had to get away from home, and do a few things

on her own. Money allowed her to make some independent decisions. Unfortunately she had no idea
how to budget her 'independence'.

*"I went down (to the West End) on my next
half day off. I had been there for another month. A
half-day off for me then was from about half past
three. I rushed all the way, with my money to
Selfridges. Sophie happened to be getting married
about this time, so I bought, not only Sophie, a
present, but also I bought everybody else in Towyn
a present. Everybody had a present. I suddenly
realised I hadn't even got money (to go) back. That's
the worst of not teaching a child to spend and save.
I hadn't got any money ever, to go back to Croydon,
let alone for the next month. So I had to go and
borrow from Llew for the next month. He gave me
two pounds."*

*"I was earning very little. It was about 25
shillings ($5) a month, if I was lucky to get that.
Even when I went to the London hospital later on,
it wasn't very much. It wasn't two pounds ($8) a
month then."*

*"Now I had two pounds, and I was to hold
this tight. I was to pay him back out of next
month . . . next month's money, and as I could.
Keeping back a little bit. Llew was teaching me
how to carry on."*

*"In the second month, Tom Jones and Llew
were coming to visit me. I'd asked permission for
them to come and I told Mrs. Efgrave. I saw them
coming down the path, and I hadn't quite finished
dressing, so she had to answer the door. Of course,
she went to the back door. As I went, she said 'Oh,
dear dear me, you should have been ready to receive your guests'. They weren't invited in the house,
but I could walk around the garden with them. So
Llew advised me. 'You want another job, better far*

than this. This is no good for you at all. Very bad place to live in. Very bad place . . . ' Very stern, old Llew was."

"I was there for two months; just over the two months. Then I gave in my notice. If you were accepted for a month you had to give a month's notice. So you'd be working to the end of the month, or forfeit your pay. Now, during this time, they had a girl from Dr. Barnardo's home and she brought a cat with her. We knew nothing about cats, and all that night that cat yelled and yelled. She crawled around all the windows and all round the bed. She crawled round all the bedrooms and all the things. She was meowing like anything and I didn't know what was the matter with thing, and she knew less. It was a queen, you see, and it was making a noise. So I said 'You can't have a cat like this.' I opened a window and the cat flew. It came back, but the girl packed her box up next day, and she went off."

Dr. Barnardo's homes were a chain of orphanages in Britain. They formed a good source of servants and labourers for the upper classes in those days, since it was felt that an orphan couldn't aspire too much and perhaps should be grateful for any position. While Dr. Barnardo must have had the well being of his charges at heart when he established his first home, the title became something of a lasting stigma.

"Mrs. Efgrave wasn't a very good woman really, although she was very smart. She said that the girl had left, having stolen things. But she hadn't stolen. Mrs. Efgrave was saving her face for her husband."

Throughout this period of service in London, Edna still had nursing in mind. Even though she got trapped into cooking and cleaning, her intentions were clear. Even in this first job she had applied first to look after the little boy. Later she found that the next best thing to nursing was to work for a doctor's family. She became a lady's maid . . . a '*tweeny*,' who could work between the servants' quarters downstairs and the family's rooms upstairs.

"*Well now, during that time I thought I'd better get away, as quick as I can. I waited until the end of that month. Then I got a job, not very far away, in Brixton, Tulse Hill. I got a job there with a doctor (Dr. Aier), now as Mrs. Aier's maid. Knowing nothing about being a lady's maid. There were children, but I didn't go in for children then. I thought I better do as my Mother told me and go into their (service). So, I went as a maid.*"

"*While I was there, there were two sons and a daughter, and Dr. and Mrs. Aier. We had a proper servants' quarters in the basement of the place, and it was very nice. I felt myself a rank up. The cook wasn't very much older than me. She was in her twenties, and she was getting ready to go abroad. She was working a few years to go to Australia. She was a very very accomplished cook. When the mistress came down with her orders in the morning, she had to leave the cook in her kitchen by ten. The mistress had to leave. They had a butler there. They had a garage man. They had an odd-job man. They had a gardener. They had a kitchen-maid.*"

"*Dr. Aier was a pathologist. He wasn't a GP; he was a Harley Street specialist . . . working with . . . what's the name of that criminologist? — Oh, dear, what was his name? . . . Oh, yes, they could afford (staff).*"

"*And it was a very beautiful house. It was*

one of these places where there was an old part in front of the house. To get to the servants' quarters you went right through a garage, which used to be a big stable. There they had one HUGE dog, and a small dog. The huge dog was with us, but the small dog was allowed to go upstairs. A small white dog. But this huge dog frightened everybody from the door. He went and flattened a postman once, absolutely flattened him (laughing). Standing over him . . ."

"We had servants' quarters there where we were allowed to invite people. When they came, they were properly dealt with. We had our own quarters and we could invite anybody. Anyway, poor old Llew when he came to visit me there, of course was terrified of the dog."

"I felt absolutely in heaven there. Now, a funny thing. My orders came through the cook to me. She said 'You'll have to go up to Madam's bedroom, and see.' 'She's going to a first night.' she said. For this first night she had a sequined frock. I managed to help her put the sequined frock on, standing up behind her. I thought it was lovely. This was the first night I'd ever helped her. Practically, the first night I was there, it was, yes. Anyway, off they went. I saw them all out and handed her cloak to her, a sort of a cape over her. Off she went. You just stood and closed the door. The butler was by my side. (I was really taking a lot of orders too from the butler, cause they were sort of initiating me into the job.) Now as soon as they went out he said 'You can go . . . it's your own time now until she comes in.' So right, we all went down stairs."

"In the cook's kitchen, when we were downstairs, we'd have our supper, you see. Proper meals, properly served, just like you were in the lady's room."

"The kitchen had plenty of room . . . Remember the old fashioned places, where we went down stairs, it was a proper suite there. Lovely furnished . . . today, it would be termed a big flat. There was like a dairy there. There was a big pantry (plenty of provisions in it) and there was our dining room. The only bedroom on that floor was the butler's. The butler did sleep on that floor. Then we had the garage . . . the driver of Mr. Aier's car; the chauffeur . . . he came in but he didn't live in. But he was not only a chauffeur, he was a man who mended all electrical lights and things like that . . . electric points, you see. A handy man, when he was not driving his master around . . . which was not very often. We always kept these things to repair for him."

"Anyway, we were all having our meals there. In the kitchen . . . we had our meals in the kitchen, on a proper table in front of a big bay window. Well now, our dinner was served after they went, after the big dinner upstairs. It was roughly speaking about half past seven, and we had properly made dinner, you know. No half measures about it. It was properly served too."

"In the cook's kitchen too the times of all our bedtimes were posted. The cook went last, next to the butler. There was the kitchen maid, (who) went early, quite early, about quarter past nine. She was . . . (you had to) go to bed. No half measures with you at all. Now my time was, roughly speaking, ten o'clock unless I was needed later."

"So this night I was needed later, to wait for Madam to come in, you see. My job was, when she came in, to be there handy by her side. She used to drop her frock on the floor. She wasn't tidy a tall. She never spoke and I never spoke to her. You couldn't speak to her. She was one of these . . . she really looked upon you as a maid."

"Now then, Madam slept in a room adjoining Dr. Aier's room. Mrs. Aier's room was . . . I'll never forget it as long as I live . . . beautiful. It had a

lovely oak bed, black oak, and her wardrobe on the
side of her room took the whole length of the side of
her room. It was all black oak. And there
were . . . let me see . . . one, two, three doors, all
open doors . . . four doors in that thing. It was
lined with more frocks than you'd seen in a
dressmaker's shop. To me who (had) never seen so
many frocks all hanging in a wardrobe — oh, I
thought I was IT, you know. Then on another side
of the room she had a small sort of cupboard arrangement, little tiny chest of drawers. These chests
of drawers kept handkerchiefs and small details.
On the other side, facing the window, she had a
flat chest of drawers, with no glass on it, but a
pearl studded glass in oak. A pearl studded glass,
which you could pick up, you know. That was her
dressing table. The table itself was black oak, you
see. And all on this black oak was a big mirror
and on the black oak dressing table was all silver,
with a crest on, an armoured leg. From here
downwards . . . an armoured leg. I was absolutely
intrigued with this dressing table. Of course, more
anxious than anything to clean it, you see. I could
see it was tarnished a bit, in some parts it was
more tarnished. In the very very corner, she had
one of these swivel mirrors . . . in the corner. Oh,
it was lovely. Adjoining her bedroom was a bathroom, into which she used to disappear."

"Now, when she disappeared into this that
night, I had run the bath for her. She disappeared.
I didn't bath her or anything. Now it was my duty
to hang her frocks, to tidy the room up, and get her
bed ready. So I did, I hung them all up dutifully.
After she came out of the bath, and as soon as she
came into the bedroom, she dropped her dressing
gown from her. It wasn't this dressing gown that
you wear today, all this nice nylon stuff and these
fine things, but they were beautiful, in real silk. So
it was easy enough to fold that and put it on a

place where she could pick it up in the morning. Then I thought, 'Now she's all ready, and I'm ready too'. I was tired the first night in a new place. So I went to bed, and she went to bed."

"Now, I used to be there in the morning to put that her dressing gown on her. My job was to take in her morning tea. Having had a sensible Mother, I now knocked on the door. No answer to come in — so I walked in, and I dutifully put the tray down and I said 'Good Morning, Madam'. She never answered, and I drew the blinds, and I said 'Good Morning, Madam'. She was wide-awake. She never said a word to me, so I went out. I just felt as if I'd been whipped. But anyway, sometime during the morning, I was called up into Madam's presence, a little later on, only to be shown this sequined frock as black as pitch. I should have wrapped it up in black paper, to stop the light getting on it. But I didn't know all this. It'll tarnish . . . and tarnish in a night. It was exactly like modern sequins but it would tarnish in a night. She told me then that I had ruined a frock worth a hundred pounds. 'Sorry, Madam, I didn't know'. I didn't know anything about it at all. She wouldn't teach you anything."

"Dr. Aier's dressing table brushes and everything were gold; all gold backed. Now in his bedroom were all these bookcases. In his bedroom you could see that he was a reader. Nobody interfered with Dr. Aier but the butler. The butler was his man, you see. When I went up with her morning tea, the butler would go up with Dr. Aier's. His was made in the room. Nothing was outside of his room. There was just a door adjoining."

"During that time, I thought her dressing tables things looked a bit tarnished, so I got a tray and dutifully took them all downstairs. Knowing only one place to clean silver, I went in the butler's pantry. I was there, and oh, Nichols went for me.

83

He said 'How dare you, how dare you, bring them down'. Well, I said, 'They want cleaning. Look at them, they want cleaning'. He said, 'Don't you dare. This is my responsibility'. I thought, then that's all right. I don't mind you doing it. He cleaned everything. But he never cleaned everything at once; he only cleaned one piece of silver, one piece of anything, per day. He did it with his thumb. You never saw anything like it. He put his thumb in powder, and it just went round . . . one thumb was straight, absolutely straight . . . he did one piece."

"They had a big old fashioned house. In the dining room there was a big square window, and in this square window was a big black wooden seat. It looked to me like a black wooden seat. In this big black wooden seat was all this silver — no end of silver pieces. On the side here was a huge cupboard, and as you opened this cupboard . . . there was all beautiful table ware . . . you've never seen anything like it. We had a speaking tube down there, and on the side of the room along the wall was the sideboard, which was a fixture, you see. All the carving knives and everything were kept there. Everything . . . fine knives, big knives."

"On the side was a table . . . everything was served . . . it came up in a lift from downstairs. Big old lift, a noisy old thing, you know. Well, it came up in the lift, and if you wanted to talk to the cook, you spoke down the speaking tube. The speaking tubes had whistles on them. We always set that table for six or for eight, even though only two sat at it. Ridiculous nonsense."

"I was there one night when there was a party on. I never really served at the table. Nichols served and I only stood behind him. Now, this night I had to do the serving to help him. I was serving and everything was . . . serve there on the right side . . . take away on the left. All this

. . . everything . . . finger bowls and everything on the table. All little lace mat arrangements (on) this black oak table. Beautiful, it was. All these shadowed lights. Lovely, and it was modern . . . when I think of that table now I think of it as modern — as a beautifully modern table to-day. I would have been 19 or 20. I was in my glory there . . . that went off beautifully. The job after the dinner . . . you cleared the dinner things and Nichols would hand me certain things. I'd put them in the lift and down they would go. We'd speak and the next course would arrive . . . very quiet he would be. Nichols was a rum case. He could make you laugh too; he really acted well. But he was really an old fashioned butler, and I was in my glory. I was happy with them."

"Now, a day or two after that, we had just a lunch. It was only Dr. Aier and Mrs. Aier, although the table was set for six. Pigeons came up. I was standing by the side of Dr. Aier, and he was telling me what knife to use for carving these little pigeons. I was watching his hands really; I wasn't even looking at the knife. With a very very sharp knife, all he used were two breasts and part of the leg, and that went on the table. None of the other (parts) of the pigeon went on, all the rest was dutifully taken down. We had the pigeons, the remains of that, and they were beautifully cooked, (that cook was a top class cook) and it was beautifully served. Remember she had help down in the kitchen."

"You don't listen to conversation (at the master and mistress's table), but this one day she wanted him to go upstairs and put a certain suit on, because he was going to Eton, his old school, to give a speech . . . opening of something or closing of something. Anyway, (laughing) he was just putting a little bit of pigeon on a fork. I can see the whole rest of this pigeon flying across the table. I'll

85

go just as I want, just as myself,' he said. 'I'll take even the suit I've got on, off. That's all they want, is ME.' You know, she didn't flicker. She was most unemotional; she was a cruel woman in a way. I wasn't supposed to listen, but I thought 'Well', but I just looked at Nichols and Nichols sort of made a face, you know. I had to run to the speaking tube, but could I say anything? I was giggling. So very suddenly, very quietly behind me . . . (softly) 'Be quiet'. Then he (Nichols) talked down the tube. Remember, I was being taught, in a way, so whatever I did wrong would be put down to that . . ."

"I was sharing a bedroom with the kitchen maid. She was a younger girl, and she was supposed to be under me. It was a lovely house really. I had my own place where I could keep my own brushes, my own dusters, and everything, and we were given a certain number of them, you see. Cook showed me this. Anyway, I knew what I had to do and I felt ever so important. It was the first really important thing I had of my own . . . but what intrigued me up in my bedroom was that I had an eiderdown. Admittedly, it was only a Paisley quilt cover; you know the type of thing, don't you? Well, it was an eiderdown and it was mine . . . I had one side of the room. Chest of drawers, and a little dressing table, and a little wardrobe (a stand-up wardrobe) and on her side she had her things, you see. We dutifully kept our own room and we had the bathroom . . . all the women servants slept upstairs in the attic."

"Half the attic was the daughter-of-the-house's nursery. That half was as big as any flat today. She had in it, in the nursery now; she had a bedroom with three single beds in it — to invite two friends in, to entertain them properly. She was about ten when I knew her. She had the nursery dining room; it was really more suitable for her when she was a young girl. I never saw her once at

*the table with her Mother and Father, although she
was ten. She had her own nurse there, and she
was a tartar. Nana, the old lady, she was an old
lady . . . she kept up there, she never ever came
down to us at all. Upstairs in her place she had
her own dresser with her own dishes, two sets of
dishes, everything from top to bottom."*

*"Yes, I was very happy there. I felt something.
I felt I was of importance, and I wasn't missing
my nursing now. I was only four months in that
job."*

But Edna was eternally curious.

*"During the first month, it was part of my
duty to see to the library in the morning and to see
to the billiard room. That was part of my work.
The library was champion, (breathlessly). It was
three-sided full of books. It had a ladder in it, a
proper library ladder. You'd climb this ladder . . . I
was sitting up on this ladder not just cleaning
down at the bottom. I was going up all the wooden
rungs, and everything I could see. And I went to
the top, and I saw a book there called* The Life of
Dr Aier. *I thought, 'Well what in the world is
this'. The man's alive!' Now, I sat on top (with)
the books, and being very fond of reading, I sat
there and forgot that time was passing by. All of a
sudden, a little man, at the foot of the (ladder)
said 'What are you doing up there?' It was Dr.
Aier. He was an early riser you see. I said 'I'm so
sorry, Sir'. 'What book are you reading?' I said*
The Life of Dr. Aier.' *'What are you reading
that for?' I said 'I'm reading because I'm wondering why it's written, because you're alive', I said,
you see (laughing). 'Well, it's about my Father.
Take that to your bedroom. Don't let anybody else
touch it, but you can read it'. I was so delighted,*

87

somehow I got off down the other side of the ladder so as not to come on his side. It was one of these ladders you can go over."

"That ladder was absolutely intriguing to me, you know. After that I knew it wasn't for my benefit at all. (Laughing)"

"Well, anyway now I got off the other side of the ladder, and said 'Yes Sir, Thank you Sir, Yes Sir'. And off I went. I'd never been used to saying 'Sir' so much. He was a little tiny ugly man."

"The billiard room seemed to me to be an annexe and oh, the billiard room was lovely. When you went in you saw this big table. It seemed to me abnormally big then, and at the end of the billiard room was an inglenook fireplace. When they used to have guests sometimes come for afternoon tea, you took the tea into this inglenook. Oh, it was beautiful. It was raised up, (with a) big huge fire. I never touched any fires. The gardener would come and light the fires in the morning, and they were continually stoked; big huge fires."

"In between the billiard room and the library was a passage, an old passage belonging to the house. In between there, there were little sheds of rabbits, and guinea pigs; they were all in this little alleyway sort of place. It was part of the house, but of course one end was an open doorway. You could open it. A morning or two afterwards, I got up and went down to the library. I was going to go to the billiard room. I see the daughter of the house . . . I forget her name . . . naughty spoilt Madam she was . . . she was now very happy. She was sitting in front of all these guinea pigs and rabbits in these cages. 'No' she says 'That one's not taken it. That one has taken it.' Having read part of this book of Dr. Aier's life . . . now I stopped to watch her. 'What do you mean?' I said. And I knelt down by her side. She was telling me all about these drugs, these drugs that her Father had given these animals. And she said 'Just look at him'. Her Father, being a pathologist, was trying things on these animals. They were not pets. She was not touching them. 'Now he's not climbing. He hasn't the energy to climb'. These cages were beautifully made. It really was a lovely thing. Now, I was well away with her, completely forgetting I had the billiard room and various other things to do before breakfast. I was easily lead (interested) by this. I was kneeling down. Then, lo and behold, Dr. Aier arrived. 'Well, do you like this?' 'Yes', I said, 'Yes, I am interested in it'. We completely forgot the billiard room. He says 'Do you understand?' 'Yes, I do' I said. Then I told him that I had a brother, a chemist . . . 'in fact two brothers', I said. And we were looking . . . 'You see this? you see that?' he said, pointing things out to me."

"Change the season . . . There was Madam one day with the gardener outside planting in between the crazy paving. I had to go past them, and I excused myself, and I passed them. I turned back to look . . . and she wouldn't look at you. I said 'Here it is, here' . . . something the gardener wanted. Before long I was helping them. Dr. Aier again came past me and he said 'Do you like gardening?' 'Yes, Sir, we've got a big garden where I lived'. And I started talking about the home garden. 'Yes, I like gardening, very much'. Then I went in and did my work."

"Soon after that came a pay day, you see. I went down for my first payday. We all had to go to the library where Dr. Aier was sitting. We all had to go separately for our money. Then he said to me . . . he was a sharp-featured fellow . . . 'Why are you in this job? What are you doing here?' . . . all the questions tumbling after each other. 'I'm in this job because I li . . . I suppose to make money . . . to have a bit of money, to earn my living', etc. etc. 'You're worth a better job than this',

89

he says. 'You get out of if as soon as you can', he said to me. 'Well, my Mother said it's better for me than nursing' 'Have you ever been nursing?' 'Yes'. 'Well, you go back to nursing . . . do anything else bar this. Take up biology, botany, or anything else, but don't do this job anymore'. He knew that the maids were treated like dirt. He never . . . although he was hard, he was one of the hardest of men, he was stern, he was a real gentleman. 'You are not fit to be in this job' he said. The way he said it meant I was fit to be in a better job. Eventually he said 'Do you understand what I mean?' 'Yes Sir'. 'Now, DO you understand?' 'Yes Sir' I said. 'You get back to nursing, get back to do nursing'. 'You get out of this as soon as you can'. 'Yes Sir, yes Sir, yes Sir' and off I went."

"Dr. Aier was father of two sons and a daughter. His eldest son, during one of these University rags, had gone off with an actress. This actress and he had got drunk, and he slept out at night with her. Next day he was so concerned about it, this young boy was, and he was going to make up to her. Live with her, you see. So . . . on the stairs, in the house was a big big break in the staircase, in the wooden staircase, and I happened to ask Rita, the cook, 'What happen here?' 'This was where Dr. Aier kicked him and his cases out'. The boy was kicked out. As he kicked the son out, and kicked his trunk behind him, (big big trunks they were) so he broke a piece off the stairs. He wouldn't allow him back either; he did wrong during one of the rags."

"The second boy . . . I forget his name the second son was supposed to be following in the steps of his Father. I met the second son. One night when they (his parents) went out, he came in . . . They had gone to one of these first nights again. While they were out, he came in and asked us if we'd dance with him. He got an old gramophone in the billiard room, and put this record on, and off we *were dancing. There was Rita, the cook; Nichols, the butler; myself and the gardener's wife came in. We had a rattling good time around this billiard table. In the middle of it Dr. Aier and his wife rang the bell and none of us moved. The son said to us 'Stand still'. He had such a voice of command, in a way that we all stood still. And Rita said 'Now we're in for it'. Nichols of course had to answer the door. Dr. Aier came in, and Mrs. Aier came in, with two friends. He said, 'See me in the morning'. We were all dismissed like that. Well, we all went to bed as meek as mild. We ought to have been in bed by our certain times. In the morning, we all went to see him. Dr. Aier was there, and he said 'Have you seen the notice (of) what time you go to bed?' 'Yes Sir'. 'Well, you haven't kept it'. 'No Sir' and all we did was say the truth . . . 'In future, keep it.'"*

"But had it been Mrs. Aier, we would have been sacked on the spot."

"During that time, Sophie, being married, lived in Kentish Town. She was the wife of a dairyman, and she'd lost a baby. She came back and she pleaded with me . . . my Mother pleaded with me . . . would I leave my job and go to her. Foolishly I did it. I had to go to her. When I arrived in Kentish Town, I'd never met my brother-in-law before. He was really and truthfully a "Steptoe' (a British Sanford'). Really and truly a 'Steptoe', a horrible man. I wasn't getting any money for this. I gave up wages. You see, Sophie found that when she got married, although he said that it was his business, it wasn't his business. So she had landed there with a Mother-in-law and a Sister, and it was their business. Tom was lazing away his time. Anyway, that's their business."

Thus, Edna left service in a very comfortable situation

to help her sister. This may have been a blessing in disguise since, with her Mother pressing her to forget nursing, her contentment in the Aier household may have taken more than a far-sighted employer's advice to break. As it was, working with her sister Sophie and her new husband Tom was an untenable situation. She had tasted the independence that working for wages had given, she had been away from her immediate family for some time, and in the back of her mind, the call to nursing was still there. First she had to leave her sister.

"I didn't go back to nursing because my Mother meanwhile was telling me not to go back to nursing. I answered an advert myself for West Hampstead for a job as a lady's maid. I was written to and told to go to my job on a Saturday, and that I would receive all my instructions from the maid whose place I was taking. I arrived there that night, and saw Mary who was leaving."

Chapter 6

Forward –
Nursing Again

'*I arrived in Tulse Hill. The girl whose place
I was taking was going to leave to get married, on the Tuesday. Mr. and Mrs. Barkley were
in Deauville, France, at the time, and were coming back on the Monday, and Mary was to leave
on Tuesday morning. I was to have all this weekend with Mary and she was to instruct me in my
job. Tulse Hill was a smaller house and not nearly
the type of house that I had left. Tulse Hill was
much better in a way. We were all now in a servants' kitchen there, not underneath, but on the
floor level. It was by the side of the other dining
room.*'

It was in this room that Edna's future was decided.

*"That first night we were all having a meal.
We were all sitting at the table. Now there was
Mary . . . four, no five of us were sitting at the
table. We were all sitting down . . . and there was
a big dresser in this kitchen, and attached to one
leg of the dresser was an Airedale, and attached to
the other were two little . . . yapping little dogs.
The old-fashioned dogs, Pekinese dogs. Two yapping little things they were. They were quiet when
we were having a meal and all of a sudden all
three dogs started barking. When the dogs barked,
Mary shouted 'Burglars burglars', and she fainted
at the other side of the table. There was a hatchway
by her side, by the dresser where these dogs were,
and one of the other girls opened the hatchway,
and she said 'Can I get on the telephone? Can I
get on the telephone?' I said 'Let's see to Mary first.'
Having had a little bit of nursing all I knew then
was to open her collar. She'd gone down completely,
and the dogs were yapping like anything; terrible
noise there was. I was new to the job and I'd hardly
taken my coat off. My case was still standing at the
door. Well, anyway, I got up and saw to her. When
she did come to she said 'I'm not going to stay here.
I'm not going to stay here. I'm going home. I'm
going home.' And she started in(to) a form of hys-
terics. I said 'You're all-right' and I shook her. I
knew what to do in that case too. I shook her, and
said 'You're all-right, there is nothing the matter
with you.' She said, 'The telephone's off, the
telephone's off.' Well, it was off. We didn't know. I
wouldn't have known anything about the telephone
as such then. Anyway, she and the other three girls
left me, a perfect stranger, in that house on my
own. They were all resident in the house. They
went and they didn't tell me where they were going,
mind you. I managed to unwind the Airedale, and
the two other dogs (they were on leads) and get a
poker in my hand. There was I standing at the*

door with a poker in my hand, not knowing what to do. Well, I thought, dash it all, they're all leaving the house. If there are burglars, what am I to do with the blooming things? Well, I was getting the dogs to safeguard me, and they were pulling me like anything, these three dogs were. I get a poker in my hand, and lo and behold! Up the path come all these girls, returning now, with a Bobby."

A Bobby, of course, is a London policeman, named for Robert Peel who started the police force. In those days, when they had regular and local beats, on foot of course, it was possible to find one quite quickly by running up the street.

"This Bobby says to me 'What are you doing with that?' 'Oh!' I said. I clutched his arm and I said 'In the name of the law, don't you leave me'. 'You have the blooming dogs, but oh, don't leave me. And I got hold of the Bobby's arm, and (laughing) walked into the kitchen. 'I'm only new here' I said, 'and you know they all ran out of the house and left me. I might have been the burglar'. Now the Bobby laughed. He had an awfully extremely funny dialect to me, but he came into the kitchen with me and the others. They were all saying they were not going to sleep there that night, but eventually it was decided that they would bring Mary's fiancé to sleep the night in the house — because they were responsible for the house."

"And if you want a policeman here . . . ' said this man, who now turned out to be a station sergeant, 'I'll send you along a policeman.' Well, seeing Mary could have her fiancé, they didn't want a policeman! But they all went off to West Norwood, funnily enough. The whole lot of them. There was no need for them all to leave. Also one of them was a Dr. Barnado girl and she went to a

95

house nearby, now leaving me, a stranger, in with this policeman."

"I cleared the table as best I could, not even knowing where anything was, and I thought . . . my Mother had always advised me not to give drink to a policeman, or to any strange man. So I turned to this policeman and I said 'Well,' I said 'I don't know whether you want a drink, but I can make a cup of tea. I wouldn't give you a drink if I had it, you know.' So this policeman said 'No, thank you, I never drink.' 'Well that's all-right', I said. Somehow or other, I unearthed a teapot and everything, and we got a cup of tea made. Now it happened to be a Jewish home, and on the table there was Jewish bread and butter. I cut some bread and butter. Well, this station sergeant was sitting there, and he got out his knife and he pushed back the poppy seeds from the Jewish bread. Me being Welsh said; 'Well, it's not dirt, you know.' I said, 'it's poppy seed.' I'd only just, about one minute before, found out that it was poppy seed. 'Jolly nice you know.' 'I don't like poppy seeds' he said in a very very broad accent. Anyway, during an hour I suppose we were there, he helped me wash-up, clear up and tidy-up and everything. He started talking about himself. He said he was going back up home to Cooomberland. I said 'Oh, dear me', it seemed awfully far away there (laughing). I didn't even know where Cooomberland was!"

"Well, anyway, he also said he was on night duty, and I was extremely sorry for him. Being of a generous nature, I only had one thing to give away . . . I had a coconut upstairs in my case. I cut up this coconut and gave him a lot of it in a paper. He put it in his pocket and said 'Thank you'. Afterwards, we went right round the house, and he showed me the house. There was no sign of a burglar, and we found that the telephone had been cut off because Madam hadn't paid her bill! He'd found that out. I don't know how he'd found that out because we couldn't get anything on the telephone, but he was the one who showed me how to use the telephone."

"When the other girls came back, he was very nice about it and assured us that he'd have a policeman outside watching. There was no burglar, and . . . Anyway, we all fell for him; every one of us fell for him. Off he went, and I was sent to my bedroom and (we) all went to bed that night."

"On the Tuesday, Mr. and Mrs. Barclay came home."

"In their house the billiard room was up on top of the house, and this billiard room was quite different to the other. It was covered with the most magnificent paintings . . . the walls were covered . . . you'd ever seen in your life, (in awe). As you came in the house first, you'd see a picture of Mrs. Barclay as if she was coming down stairs. Then when you went upstairs in all the rooms there were beautiful pictures. There was one striking one upstairs of a gypsy, jet-black hair, all coloured rags on her, carrying a baby. Even this baby looked gypsylike. Although it was a baby . . . with little children behind and all the coloured rags you could find . . . It was really exquisite. Then there was another one . . . more like a Spanish lady (with) her hair very high on her head. Well, anyway, I was very intrigued with these pictures. Mr. Barclay soon found out, and when (he found) I came from Wales, he asked me—did I love pictures? I said 'Yes, I do.' He asked me did I know of any wealthy people in Wales. I said 'I don't know any, I'm from poor people who couldn't afford to buy pictures.' Mr. Barclay was a dealer in pictures."

"Mr. Barclay's cousin was Josie Collins, of Maid of the Mountains. I met her. They called

97

*me up to meet her. I served tea to her in their own
private little room."*

*"Anyway, one thing lead to another and I was
very dissatisfied there because Mr.
Barclay . . . Every Jew wants a lot of children. Now
I didn't know at the time when I went there that
there was discord between the husband and wife,
because she would not have children, and he
wanted a family. So he went elsewhere for a family, and there was a divorce brewing. But I didn't
know all about this."*

Without being apologetic about it, generic myths
about the Jewish people have abounded throughout Europe from time immemorial. Edna's views were
perhaps uneducated (there are very few Jews in Wales
outside of the larger towns), but they were not big-
oted views. Neither she nor her employers apparently thought twice about, on one hand of being hired
into a Jewish home or on the other of hiring a gen-
tile to help care for them.

*"During that time, it became one of my duties
to take these three dogs out. I hated it like anything, because I'd never been used to heat, standing by dogs. I used to have a white overall in the
morning when I walked them. It was also my duty
to go for two rashers of bacon. No Jewess is allowed
to eat bacon. But I was allowed to go, with these
dogs, for a walk and to bring two rashers of bacon
home. They were for Madam's breakfast!"*

*"One day when I was going out, a man was
standing on the corner of the road. I had been very
strictly brought up. Not strictly either, but my Mother
always used to say 'Don't you talk to strange men,
and keep your head well up and look straight in
front.' Well, the advice has cost me an awful lot of
falls, but anyway I walked straight on in front,*

*and I heard this man say to me 'And when can I
give YOU a coconut?' I walked straight past him,
and I thought 'Of all the cheek!' I dutifully pulled
the dogs where they wanted to stop, and I (laughing) . . . got the bacon. When I was coming back,
the same man was on the corner of the road again.
He had a cape on. He was in uniform. He said
'Aren't you going to let me give you some coconut?'
Then, I suddenly thought 'It's my policeman!'"*
        "By this time we had all beer and funning (in
the kitchen). They were teasing me for staying in
the evening with him, but they left me, didn't they?
'Can't you write to him?' The next day they had all
dared me to phone when the telephone came back
on. He'd said we could ask for a policeman, so I
went on the telephone . . . 'I don't mind'. We
phoned to ask for our 'Crown Sergeant'. He wasn't
a 'Crown Sergeant'. We only knew that he had a
mustache and a crown on his sleeve. That was a
Station Sergeant, but we didn't know anything
about the police. So somebody answered on the telephone, and I said 'Is the Crown Sergeant there?
We'd like to speak to the Crown Sergeant, please.'
'Crown Sergeant? No, our Crown Sergeant is away,
Madam.' 'Well, he said we could ask for a policeman.' 'Do you want a policeman?' 'No, thank
you.' . . . and we put it down quick
(laughing) . . . we were so frightened . . . we
wanted THE policeman."
        "Well, anyway, when this man on the corner
of the road asked me could he give me some coconut, 'No, it's chocolate I like.' Off I went home,
very quickly now . . . bouncing on the other girls,
saying 'I met my Crown Sergeant, I met my Crown
Sergeant.' (If I'd seen his crown and sergeant
(stripes) I might have recognized him.) Anyway,
next morning when I was coming down
stairs . . . first thing in the morning, lo and behold, the letter box opened and down dropped a*

99

parcel . . . *without any name on. I ran to the
kitchen. My job was to give the letters in to the cook
and the cook put them in a certain place for the
master and mistress. I ran in, 'There's a parcel
here. I'm sure it's my box of chocolates, I'm sure it's
one . . . it looks like a box . . . '. We twisted it round
in our hands and we dared each other to open it.
It wasn't addressed to anybody, so we opened the
box. Lo and behold, it was Nestles Milk Chocolates. A blue box it was then."*

"A day or two after that, I was asked by Mr.
Barclay – (if there were any letters) addressed to
Mrs. Barclay: I should put them with his and he
would give me five bob (shillings) a week more. So
I put all the letters on his tray. Now Mrs. Barclay
asked me quietly, would I keep any letters I saw
coming in the post addressed to Mr. Barclay for
her. So I dutifully passed them over (laughing): he
had hers, and she had his! I was getting five bob
from each. I was getting ten bob. Now the postman
knew all about it, because he'd been asked too. I
said 'I've never seen such people. What's the matter with them?' 'Huh huh,' he said, 'you know.'"

"Now this postman was as young as I was.
He was very keenly interested in football, and I
said 'Ooh, so am I' I only knew that my Father
wore a football jersey, in a picture at home. I said
'I'm interested . . . ' I'd been once to a football
match with my Father, and I'd shouted 'Kick it,
Tom, kick it, Tom.' When this postman said he
was interested in football I said I was interested.
So he invited me out on a Saturday afternoon.
The first Saturday afternoon I was to go to tea
with his Mother, and then we'd go to a football
match. So I said 'Yes.' He was pretty safe. I knew
him: he was coming to the door, wasn't he? So I
went to the football match with him, and his Mother
was a very nice little woman, you know. Very ordinary. I went to the football match and thoroughly

enjoyed myself. Came home, early, you know. Cause
I was only told to go out to the football match and
back, and he was pretty annoyed. "

Young ladies in service were very restricted in
their time off. Edna had previously had one afternoon a month, and so each occasion loomed high
on the horizon and in the memory. They were generally occasions for much pre-planning and if a young
man was in the offing then so much the better. Still,
young ladies knew that their eventual prospects depended on marriage, since being in service was not
a life long prospect for most. 'Young men' then, came
from the staff, or the tradesmen, or possibly from a
church congregation. The excursion to the football
match was typical of first outings, although the postman must have been quite a serious character to in-
clude his Mother in his first afternoon with Edna.

"During that time, Dadda came up to London
and he went to stay with Sophie in Kentish Town.
I was to go and meet them (at) King's-Cross Chapel
on Sunday. I had to go to Swiss Cottage from West
Hampstead, and pick up a bus there. I missed it
as usual, so I turned round. 'It's no good, I can't
get to . . . ' Never thought of getting another bus. I
could easily have got one, or I could have got the
underground, but I didn't know anything about
that. Anyway I thought, I'll go to chapel round
here. Now, I didn't know where the chapels were,
so I was wandering along and it looked like the
starting of a service in this hall — so I walked in.
It was a little mission hall . . . and I walked into
this place. You know how sensitive I am to new
places, least I was . . . so I went in this place and
sat on the back seat and I immediately started cough-
ing. They were starting to pray, and I put my head

101

down. Then, fumbling right in front of me was what I thought was a sixpence being pushed towards me. You know how you put your head down like that and I saw this sixpence . . . so I pushed the sixpence back, and I heard somebody say. 'It's peppermint, it'll stop your coughing.' So I looked up, and to my horror, it was my policeman! By my side, you see, (giggling) now dressed differently again. I daren't look . . . I blushed . . . and he handed me the peppermint. When the time came to sing I ate that peppermint; it was a little tiny tiny one. We had to share the hymnbook, but could I sing? Not a sound . . . I couldn't think . . . (laughing) 'Jesu, Lover of my Soul.' I couldn't sing a thing. Then we went through the service, and he asked me 'Can I walk home with you?' 'Yes, you can if you like.' I didn't dare say 'No.' To begin with, it was dark and I didn't know the way home. I felt I was safer with him. So we walked home, and we went straight home too. We didn't lollick (lollygag) about, anyway."

"We made arrangements then to go to the pictures, next time off. Only the cinema it was. I don't remember a bit about the pictures; not one bit. I don't even remember seeing the picture (laughing). Honest . . . It was THE GILDMAN it was. I only remember a big high seat; high up somewhere we had to go with a lot of old stairs. I felt, oh, terrible and he was helping me everywhere. I'm sure I must have dragged, going up those steps. I didn't dare tell the girls . . . Funny thing I never told the girls about this. Now we came out, and we had to go somehow out by the back of the cinema to come into the road. Now my Bobby was talking. His accent was quite different to anything I knew — very very Cumberlandish, really North Country. Mind you, he'd been in London about fourteen years. Anyway, he was talking and it suddenly dawned on

me . . . I was reading a notice on the wall . . . it
said

THE POLICE HAVE AUTHORITY TO TAKE INTO CUSTODY ANYBODY FOUND WANDERING HERE.

"Now, I giggled. I could see a funny side . . . me walking with him, and him talking, you see, and I laughed. He just said (grimly) nothing. We went out and we walked home. (He didn't notice what I was laughing at.) I never said a word, I just laughed you see, and he never said a word. He said nothing. He was annoyed, but I didn't know at the time. He was very polite, you know. And after I came home, I thought 'Dash it all, we never made any appointment to go . . .', to go out with him, you see. I thought 'What in the world have I done?' I went in. I was as calm as anything that day. Never said anything to the girls, and off I went to bed. I thought 'I wonder what I have done wrong? I wonder what he-was saying when I saw that thing (notice).' That thought came to me: 'I wonder what he was saying?'"

"Then, during this time, there was disagreement between the husband and wife, and cousins in the house. I was fed up with it . . . fed up with service . . . fed up to do the moods of one man. Mr. Barclay was exceedingly nice to me, and she was exceedingly nice to me. But she brought a male cousin in to watch him, and he brought his girl cousin in to watch her! That's the gospel truth. Now the man cousin, her man cousin was a nasty young man . . . he was a really horrible man . . . to whom I had to take a poker and hit him! That's the type of man he was. Well anyway, I thought I'm not going to stay here."

"I was responsible for a sink in the pantry.

That sink was made like one of these cardboard sinks so that you didn't break dishes. In the servants' quarters, there, in the pantry, were two sinks. Anything from the table in the way of fine china came through my hands, and I was responsible for washing it in the protective sink. When I went in one day this Dr. Barnado girl, a new one was washing her apron in my sink. Now you don't ever use soap in that type of sink . . . it was for rinsing, only for rinsing. No strong soaps at all. You didn't dare use it . . . and she had soda in it! Now I fought, literally fought with her, to get her out. She fought with me and during the schmozzle Mr. and Mrs. Barclay came in. It was a small house! They came in and called me 'Mary' (after the other girl that had left), 'Mary, Mary, I never knew you had a temper.' 'Yes, I've got a temper' I said. 'She shan't do it . . . You made me responsible, Mrs. Barclay, for this, Madam, for this sink, and she was washing her aprons in it.' We had fought so much that she tore my clothes and I tore hers too. I said 'I'm going back. I'm not going to stay in service. I don't like service.' Then he came to me . . . he tried to take me out of the room to talk to me quietly. I said 'No, I don't want to stay here. It's not a place for me. I'm going back to my nursing. I'm going to nurse. I'm going to nurse.'"

"I asked 'Can I use your telephone?' So I telephoned Llew. (He was in Gloucester Place in Kensington now) Would he come for me, I can't stand this place. I said it on the telephone, in front of them. Meanwhile . . . 'Will you ask him to come over, and let us meet him?') 'Yes, you can meet my brother.' Then Llew was manager of the Chemist's or Pharmacy Department in Gamages in London. When Llew said 'You don't talk like that to anybody.' I said 'No. I don't. But I'm not employed by them now. I'm leaving to-night.' 'Now, you can't leave to-night like that unless you lose a month's

*money.' So I worked my time up there, then I went
to Llew's."*

During her initial years in London, Edna's brother
Llewellyn, eleven years her senior, was a rock to which
she could retreat when things got too much. He was
a quiet solid character, with quiet humour, and very
dependable. He had standing through his chemist's
training and his senior pharmacist's position where
he worked. Very shortly he was to marry a Miss Doris
Gems of Wigmore Street.

Doris Gems' mother was a Royal Court dressmaker with 40 girls under her. The association with
King Edward VII made them upper middle class and
so Doris had been raised with a nanny and had been
taught by a governess. Her nanny, a Miss Edwards,
later moved to Greece to work with the Royal family
there. She helped to raise a small boy who was later
to become the Duke of Edinburgh, consort of Queen
Elizabeth II. In the 1970's, Miss Edwards at age 91
was reported in the national press to be helping two
writers to document the Duke's early years. Half a
century later there is still enough class-consciousness
in Britain that these associations are important. They
were even more important in 1925. Llewellyn was
doing well for himself.

Although Edna kept nursing in mind throughout these years and relied on her own ability more
and more, the fact that she could get help as close as
a phone or a short bus-ride away must have been
strengthening. She was not quite independent, even
though she probably could have managed if forced.

*"During these few days, I didn't meet the po-
liceman at all. During that time Mr. and Mrs.*

105

Barclay did all they could and offered me all kinds
of money. I think I had three rises in less than a
month! Now my money was going up. However, I
said I was going to nurse: 'I don't care what anybody says, I'm going back to nursing.'"

"I hadn't any money as such to pay for my
training. In the olden days you could go to St.
Mary's of London for 20 pounds a year. I hadn't
got it. I hadn't got anything. I was under the im-
pression (that) you couldn't even ask for it. Llew
did offer to send me there. I said 'No, I'm not going
to go anywhere were I've got to pay back money. I'm
going to go somewhere where I can stand on my
own feet.' I applied to St. Peter's Hospital London. It was again a sort of a poor law institution
outside the London Hospital . . . on the other side
of the road."

"Anyway, I went to stay with Llew for a time,
not having seen the postman nor the policeman
anymore. In fact, it didn't concern me at the time,
you see."

"The night before I was due to go to the hospital for an interview, one of the maids in the house
where Llew was staying came to Llew . . . I was
sitting in the bedroom with him. She said 'A Gentleman to see, Miss Morgans.' I shuddered. I thought
'Good Heavens, who's to see me?' I was too nervous to talk to strangers. If anybody looked at me,
I ran. But anyway, to my horror who turned up
but the Bobby! I said to Llew 'Oh, this is Mr. Graham.' And Llew and he became fast friends. They
really liked each other from the beginning."

"Now Llew was engaged to the girl of the house.
I think we were preparing to go out. We went round
Kensington Gardens for a walk, so Llew went with
his girl and Robert (as the Bobby was called) came
with me. I said to him the first thing 'How in the
world did you find out where I was? I never told
you, I never told anybody.' 'No, but you've forgot-

ten. I'm a policeman. 'Wherever you go I'll follow you', he said. 'Well,' I said, 'Tomorrow, I'm going to St. Peter's Hospital as a nurse. I'm going to do my training.'"

"Llew had given me instructions to St. Peter's Hospital, but Mr. Graham offered. 'I'll take your sister to St. Peter's Hospital.' There was a taxi at the door in the morning, and off we went."

"We had time now, mind you, to talk at the other end, and Robert pleaded with me NOT to go into the Hospital! He wanted to run away and get married straight away. He told me that he had already proposed to me coming out of the cinema! I said 'I didn't know that you were asking me to get married' (laughing) I said 'I was looking at the notice on the wall.' 'Yes', he said, 'you were very rude.' 'But,' I said, 'Oh, I'm not ready to get married.' I said 'I'll have to ask my Mother.'"

'Oh', I said, 'I'm not ready to get . . . and even if . . . St. Peter's . . . Oh, No, I didn't dare get married then.' Well, he said if I liked he'd take me down to Sutton, and we could get married before his brother, a minister. 'Oh no, not anywhere away from my Mother.' (My Mother would have to come to my wedding, and we had to do it properly if I was going to be married.) My Mother liked a wedding in Towyn chapel, I said, and in white. That's what my Mother liked. Sophie'd been married during the time I was up in London, and I would be the third (daughter). 'Oh no, no, it had to be done properly.' Everything had to be done because of Mamma, you see. I wasn't thinking about myself . . . and I haven't got any money for clothes, you know. So he said 'I'll buy you clothes.' 'No,' I said, 'I don't take . . . oh, no . . . No woman takes any money from any man.'

Robert Graham was born in a small stone farm,

'Lunnon', on the hills above Nenthead, itself the highest village in England. The town straddled the Pennine ridge in Cumberland; small white stone buildings set on the bleak moors and swept by salty winds from the Irish Sea. The sheep roaming the uplands as well as a little Scottish cattle rustling originally supported Nenthead's population. By the end of the 19th century even this remote outpost became part of the Industrial Revolution. Lead had been found in the hills. Lead mines scarred the area with ugly waste tips. Robert's destiny there, if not sheep, was the mine. He spent two years as an apprentice dry-stone-wall builder but then, as a young boy, he entered the mine as a donkey-engine minder. The donkey engine worked the vital pumps that kept the mine dry. They needed care day and night. The combination of subterranean darkness, rats and boredom

Lunnon

drove Robert to apply to the London Metropolitan Police. This was unheard of in Nenthead. The day he left, the first young man to leave the village for the capital, the whole population turned out to wish him well. In London, he and the Police suited each other. He got on well, rising rapidly through the ranks.

When he met Edna, he was eleven years her senior, the same age as her brother Llewellyn. This probably explains why they got on so well together . . . they were contemporaries. Robert had also been married before, to a consumptive bride. She had died in less than two years. To Edna then, here was an imposing man, who despite his country upbringing, was a man of the world, and knowledgeable in the ways of London. He was sufficiently her senior not to brook much delay in their relationship. Furthermore he had the advantage of almost being able to step into the shoes of her reliable brother, Llewellyn, to become her protector. In retrospect, she may not have stood a chance!

Still . . .

"Anyway, I went to St. Peter's Hospital. Of course, outside St. Peter's is a very ugly old place really, but once you not in it you felt you were someone. Once I got in any hospital . . . well, I felt I was someone. There was a step up, you see, and I was quite happy when I got there."

"I was very keen on my nursing and I was very keen on my Sister Tutor work (studying). During that time in the hospital, I decided not to be an ordinary nurse: to be either a theater sister whom I thought was wonderful, or a sister tutor. I liked writing, and I liked nursing."

"I thought the sister tutor had a darned easy job. She had to take complaints. All she went round was making mischief. That's all I could see . . . I

109

remember once, my duty and my instructions from one of the sisters were that I was to open alternate windows daily. If one time it was alternate one way, then next time it was reversed. It so happened there was one patient in that one ward that was bedridden. She was a young girl. She was in a high bed, very high she was, and she had been there a long time, although she was only young. Now she said 'You don't open my windows.' Well, I'd had my instructions from the Sister, so I didn't take any notice of her. When the Sister Tutor came up, the young girl told Sister Tutor that she'd already told me that I wasn't to have that window open, and the Sister Tutor, to my horror . . . disgraced me in front of the whole ward, in front of this patient. So I didn't like the Home Sister . . . mind you, I thought it was an easy job, she was doing. She was going round taking all complaints, and, my gosh, she would rectify them. You had to do things right."

"Remember it was much harder in this poor-law training. Even then we weren't allowed to touch a syringe or an injection needle or anything until the first year was up. The other year in Liverpool didn't count. Oh, no no. It didn't, not a bit. The only way it counted was that I'd had more (experience), and by this time I was older. I was more conversant with things. I knew what to do with bedpans, and all these small details of a hospital. I knew how to make a bed. Making a bed today is nothing as strict and as stern, or as clean in many ways though everything is easier done, sterilized quicker . . . But anyway, I enjoyed it then too."

"During the time I was there, Robert and I were corresponding. I also made the stipulation that I was never going to get married to him, or even engaged, I said, until talked to my Mother. I said, 'My Father's got very good furniture. He's got a bevel-end bed.' (Laughing) Then one day I

was called to the phone, 'Mr. Graham to talk to
you, nurse.' He said 'Are you due out for your two
hours? I've found the bevel-end bed.' I was to come
and see it — an 'Ottzman', mind you, that bed
came from. 'Ottzman'. My gosh! That's the one (we
ended up having at home). When I saw it, in order to get out of agreeing to get married, I said the
bevel wasn't going the right way (laughing). You
see my Father's bevel-end bed was made out of two
old canopy bedsteads; the top was flat, but the bevel
at the bottom curved upwards. It had two big post-
ers on it. I even drew it for Robert. I knew he
couldn't get one."

"All this time, Robert was agitating for me to
leave. Eventually, I promise . . . I got engaged. I
don't remember the date . . . "

"He went up home to Nenthead. While he was
there he wrote and (quietly) told me that he hoped
I was being true to him, and all the rest of it: that
he'd heard from a policeman that I wasn't true. So
I just took my ring off my neck. (No nurse was
allowed to wear jewelry.) I told him to take it back:
that I wasn't going to have anyone watching me. I
was very indignant about it really. Another time,
he was agitating to get married quickly, and I wasn't
really ready for it. 'No,' I said, 'I'm going to finish
my training.' I even gave him his ring back a second time. I didn't even put it in an envelope. I
threw it at him. (Laughing) He had to search for
it. But the making up was all-right afterwards!"

"Thomas from Cornwall came with Llew to
see me and met Robert at the same time. All three
visited me at St. Peter's one afternoon."

"Something else happened while I was nursing, and this is what really tipped the scale. Sophie
had had a child. This first child had died, and,
being sister-like, I felt I ought to go and see her the
next two hours (off). I refused to see Robert for this
once. A friend of mine, a Nurse Wass was going

111

out with a boy. She was only my age . . . 'Going out' then meant only that we looked at each other sort of thing. She said, 'If you see . . . outside then, will you tell him I can't come.' So I went and saw him, and said 'Nurse Wass can't come this afternoon.' She had the next little bed to me. So she couldn't come, and the young man said 'Which way are you going?' I said, 'I'm going to West Hampstead' . . . (It was then, part of West Hampstead) 'to see my sister.' Now it turned out that this man was a busman, so he said 'Oh. I'll take you over.' So he kindly took me over."

"I went to the nursing home where Sophie was. I was shown this little baby. Exactly like Trevor it was. The first baby that Sophie had died, and now this was the second baby who also died. They took me to see the dead baby in another room. They had a proper burial for that one. Well, after being with Sophie. I went back to St. Peter's. The young man who took me to this hospital was on the other side of the road. We just jumped on the bus . . . on a tram, I think, part of the way, and we went back to the hospital. I told Nurse Wass that I'd met him and that he'd taken me down and back, and that was that."

"Two days after that I was called to Matron's office. Sophie had been in the window . . . (She was in bed when I saw her) . . . she'd gone to the window to wave me away. I hadn't looked up and she'd seen me meet a strange man and get on a tram. So she wrote to the hospital and told the Matron that she ought to watch what I was doing in my spare time. And I had visited her! I told the Matron what had happened, and that was that. She said 'But in the porter's lodge three men visited you last week?' I said, 'Yes, they did.' 'Who were they?' And I said then, 'A Gentleman who I am going to get married to (and I never thought about it before) Mr. Graham, Mr. Morgans, my brother from Cornwall, (and) Mr. Morgans, my brother from London.' I said, 'To verify this you can phone to Mr. Graham in West End Lane (Police Station). You can phone to Mr. Morgan in Gamages. The awful part wasn't the Matron. She was awfully nice about it. I said 'You mustn't take too much notice of my sister because somehow or other I get into trouble all the time with her' I told her that she had lost the baby."

"She was really not right in her head from the baby. She made an awful time for me. The questions that were asked me were appalling. I was old enough but I didn't stand up for myself. I wrote and told my Mother at the time what had happened. They phoned to Llew. Matron had to phone to Llew, and had to phone to Robert, and poor old Robert came up. Daddy came up and he clinched the matter by saying 'Come on, let's get out of it. You mustn't stay in a place like this.'"

Save us from well meaning religious maniacs. Sophie had been the bane of Edna's life on more than one occasion prior to this, and as it turned out, later as well when she became a 'Jehovah's Witness.' Now she had effectively cut Edna's nursing career short by making it so uncomfortable that marriage looked like a better opportunity.

"When a girl joins a poor law (institution) she signs a form whereby she promises to stay after her probationary period of two months for four more years. Well, I had finished my probationship, but I hadn't signed anything. It was fortunate for me that I hadn't signed. Before you leave, you go and have an interview before the committee, sort of thing. It's one of these round table conferences. One man asked me was there any real hurry to get married? Why was I leaving to get married? Was

there any real need, or hurry to get married? I said
'No, there's no hurry to get married.' . . . and I
stopped. The medical superintendent said 'I think
you need an apology, don't you nurse?' I said 'Yes.'
I didn't know what he was talking (about) . . . you
see how naive people can be. So he said, 'I'm sorry
Nurse.' He asked me if I'd signed a form to stay
there. I said 'I've signed no form.' Did I feel that
the man I was marrying needed me more than the
hospital people? Didn't I think it was
avocation . . . a calling? I said, 'Yes, I love my
patients. I'm very happy with them.' Well, did I
feel I loved my husband, the man I was going to
get married to? I said 'Yes, much more.' I nearly
said 'Now', but I didn't dare because Matron was
there, you see. I was called in a little later on to
speak to Matron in her office and for Matron to
speak to me. She was awfully nice about it. She
said 'Couldn't you wait a year or two?' But I said
'Mr. Graham doesn't want to wait a year or two.
Neither of us wanted to wait a year or two.'"

"That's when I left."

"During that time, the Wembley Exhibition of
1924 was on. I wouldn't get married to Robert. I
wouldn't really finalise anything until my prospec-
tive husband saw my parents. It happened that
they were coming up . . . (to the) Wembley Exhibi-
tion. My Mother and Father were staying with
Sophie."

"It was on Sophie's birthday. We were wishing
her 'Happy Birthday' and I said 'Would you
like . . . Can I bring Mr. Graham over to see you?'
She said, 'You know I won't have anybody here
until I know his strict intentions.' (I did know
then, quietly.) So Robert said 'No, we won't go and
see her.' Robert wouldn't meet them there. He wanted
to meet her parents alone."

"My sister, Jane Mary was up with them, and
so Jane Mary and Robert took them on top of a bus

to Wembley. Robert took charge of us, and he pleased my Mother and Father very much by putting my Mother in a wheel chair, (though she was only 61.) For elderly people you used to push a wheel chair around these exhibitions. The wheel was fixed in the front so that a hired pusher was needed to do it. It happened to be a big Negro that was wheeling her round. There was nothing my Mother liked better. And every time she looked up she could see this man smiling. Robert got round Mamma very well . . . every time we'd stop to eat or drink poor Mamma was sitting in the chair. She'd never been so well cared for in all her life. Dadda was very thoughtful because although she wasn't an invalid, she couldn't have walked all that way. We walked round and we sat . . . for a picture of us standing under some statuette outside the exhibition. We looked awful really, (laughing) looking back at it, but we were extremely happy when we were sitting there. Poor old Dadda was in his element in the Wembley Exhibition. Robert did everything for them. When he wanted to, he could be absolutely top-notch. Then he took us all home, and he left outside the door. He wouldn't even go inside to see Sophie. He was right."

"When I left St. Peter's, I spoke to Mamma about getting married and she said 'Oh, you don't get married yet. You must stay home for a time.' So I went home, and I waited about a month until October . . . we had spoken, Robert and I . . . He wanted to get married on the date he joined (the police) which was October 25th. Well, I didn't know as much about marriage as my Mother did, and she said 'No, you can't get married.' But anyway, we GOT married on October 24th! While I was home, we passed a letter from each other every day. You see there were ten and a half years between Robert and I."

"Robert was ten and a half years older than

me. Of course, my Father thought that because of that age difference I would feel it in later years. We never felt it at all . . . all my life. Not as Dadda tried to say. Because we were very suitably matched in many ways. I had a temper, and he had a temper, but they were tempers that balanced things a bit (laughing). It was a good thing. It doesn't harm people to have a will of their own."

"Robert was extremely shy, and Dadda would tease me all the time. I was getting everything ready. I think they got me ready. I don't ever remember . . . Sophie did ONE thing for my wedding, which I have never forgotten. She was going by bus to Blythe Road . . . I often call it the Blythe nightdress really . . . she stitched two pieces of silks together and this silk must have been very very narrow. She stitched this by hand. She's the only one that had had sewing lessons. It was supposed to be my wedding nightdress . . . (Laughing). It split right down . . . (Laughing) . . . it split right down the middle. Never saw such a sight in all your life, on the wedding night. So much for Sophie's gifts. They were never any good."

"Before I left London we were trying to buy my wedding garment. Robert was very persuasive when he wanted his own way. We stood in front of Peter Robinson's one evening, and the window was dressed up with a wedding. There was the bride in a beautiful white frock. It was a beautiful frock, in double material. 'I haven't got any money to get married in. (It's) no good.' I said. 'I can't get married. I've no money.' I did have 13 pounds saved, since I resold my nursing uniform. I said, 'I haven't got money to buy that thing.' 'Those are only for looking at. Poor people can't buy that. Well, he walked me into that shop and you can believe it or not, I tried that wedding frock from the window of Peter Robinson's, and he bought it! He said 'Look when a man gets married to a girl, he's got to keep her. Many men keep them

before they get married.' Well I said, 'I'm not.' (Laughing) I came out of Peter Robinson's not knowing what he had done really, but broken hearted, as if I'd fallen by the wayside (giggling). He'd bought the frock. It wasn't to be sent to me, mind you, but sent to home."

"All arrangements were made by letter when I was at home at Towyn . . . 'Oh' I said, 'No, I'm not going to have nothing but red roses.' Being October I had bronze chrysanthemums for table decoration and the bridesmaid, Ria. I know Sophie wasn't asked to be a bridesmaid. They were all there. Bar one and that was the one I really wanted, because she could have understood more about dressing (than anyone). That was Gretta."

"The wedding morning arrived, pouring with rain. I was looking outside. Now I wasn't worrying whether it was raining or not. I knew I was going to get married; getting out of it all. You see. I wasn't worried at all about the rain. In comes Gretta, and she kneels by my bedside, and she sobs her heart out. . . . In my little bedroom, mind you. The worst little bedroom in the house I was in then. But it was . . . you know it was MY bedroom. I liked it. I said, 'Oh, I'm glad you've come.' And we both cried like anything. She was crying because she was remembering her own wedding day, and how soon she had lost her husband. She wasn't crying because she was going to lose a little sister."

"She was only crying because she was remembering her own wedding. I remember saying in the middle of the tears . . . 'Anyway he's in uniform.' (Laughing) Her husband had been in 'uniform'. He was a chief engineer on (the) sea. Robert didn't get married in uniform, but I wanted to tell her that he was a uniformed man."

"Robert came the night before, but he wasn't allowed to stay at home. Not likely! He was taken next door. We had a lot of people staying round there,

117

and to my horror, the one I didn't want at my wedding, Katie Felin, came and gave us a set of tea knives with yellow handles. They are pretty good, but I never liked them. I was absolutely wild . . . oh, I didn't want her in the wedding. That was the only discord in my wedding. I was wild that Mamma had even asked her."

"All the family were there. It's very vague. Can you remember much of your wedding? All I do remember . . . this . . . we went up to . . . let me see . . . we went up to (the) Corbett Hotel, Maria and I did, for some flowers for decorations. They even got us snowdrops and red roses . . . red roses and snowdrops . . ."

"None of Robert's (family) came. He was all alone. It was a shame really. He even offered to pay for them. He did everything he could, but they wouldn't come. Mind you, they came and interviewed me while I was courting him (indignantly) to see that I was suitable. There's was a family."

"We went back to the little home we were going to make in Cricklewood for our honeymoon. We were jolly glad to get back, mind you . . . He'd got this nice mahogany bedroom suite for me; he got nice oak furniture; leather chairs we still have got (forty years on) . . . he bought well. We had a bedroom with blue tiles on the window, and I had blue lace curtains. I had pink in our own living room. Then we had a kitchenette. That was our flat in Cricklewood, in a brand new house, in front of a little church. We were absolutely happy there."

So Edna was married. She had survived the encounter and inspection by Robert's family and he had survived the battle with Sophie and charmed Edna's parents magnificently. In those days the families were close and self-protective. Both Edna and Robert were each one of ten children . . . close protective siblings. Now they had to look after each other alone.

Chapter 7

Marriage to the Metropolitan Police

Even though Edna appears now to have made the break with her family circle, and to have emerged, for real, into the world, she has not become independent. Marriage in the first half of this century was not 'emancipated' in the way of the second half. It was a comfortable institution in which the wife followed and cared for her husband, while he took the place of her parents in making the decisions. Edna however has moved into a double marriage . . . since Robert himself was comfortably married to the London Metropolitan Police in the same way. Just as Robert made decisions for his wife, Edna, so the Metropolitan Police made decisions for

119

Robert. These ranged from where he should live, how he should live . . . and even, with whom he should live. At an earlier time, Robert had defied the Police authorities in marrying his first consumptive wife. After her death, presumably now young and healthy Edna was acceptable. Still the influence of the Police was not yet apparent.

"Soon after the wedding, Robert actually took me to the bank and started a banking account for me. We walked down to the bank and, even though I didn't have a bank account, he doubled my money. You know I broke my heart, because I was again receiving money. I never thought that he was to give me money. You know you don't really think. It's all a new life, isn't it? I signed myself 'Edna Morgans'. I had to re-sign myself, 'Edna Graham', with a signature underneath. It really frightens you at first."

Despite the romance and the excitement, Edna moved into a dependent state that frightened her, even though neither she nor Robert recognized it for what it was. They were no different from their parents or from the thousands of other married couples around them. Edna's attempt at independence had come to an end and she needed to find other measures of success.

"Robert was in Kilburn, West End Lane, by now. I found the change from a working girl to the wife of a man on shift duty hard? I did, in so much that I had so much time. I had to go back to doing what I had been doing as a child, cleaning and polishing a brand new flat . . . Our flat was very small . . . an upstairs flat in another person's house. Kitchenette, bedroom, and sitting room-cum-dining room.

So now I had three rooms that I polished and polished and polished and polished. You've never seen such polishing in all your life. We only had rugs and the linoleum belonged to the tenant downstairs. Really and truly I was polishing their lino, and there was no need for me to polish. But . . . what I missed more than anything was the freedom. I had a sudden sort of feeling that I was enclosed in those three rooms, with Robert away on the shift work. But I hadn't really been free before, so it was a very happy time, waiting for him. Eventually we were to have 12 years in London. We always said . . . 12 years before we left to go back to Wales."

"(The first child) came in about the first 10 months. We were married in October (1925) and Jean was born the following August. During those months I hadn't really gone out much on my own in London, I was waiting in the house. These were the early days of wireless, and Robert used to make these cat's whiskers wirelesses, and all these little electrical things . . . that's what he used to like . . . oh, his hobby was wireless, and anything with pencils. He used to go to shops where they sold pens and pencils, and writing materials. He used to stay for hours there. So if I went shopping, he'd either go to a newspaper and stationery shop, or a shop where there was wireless, you see. I looked at more blueprints of these wirelesses than anything (else), even when we were in Wembley before we got married. It was a wireless blueprint that we saw there. Robert was very keen in his pastime. When I would buy myself a sixpenny pocket library book, he would invariably buy a book on making up blueprints. He would love making things that had a lot of these connections . . . like wirelesses. He was very very tidy, extremely tidy. I didn't even have to cleanup after him. Besides the cat's whiskers sets we had a proper radio, a smaller type it was. Well, small then."

121

Characteristics descend through the ages in more than facial shapes and images. Robert's son, and later his grandson, were both also entranced with pens and paper, and in the currency of the times, with electronics (wireless.) In a reverse fashion, if Robert had lived in an age of computers, he too would have been a 'Mac person.'

"We were there in that house a very short time. We were very uncomfortable there really. They were so house-proud . . . The landlady knew before I did practically that we were going to have a child, so, she was throwing us out, you see. Night after night, while I was pregnant, we were looking for another home. It's pretty grim, looking for a house then, especially in the winter. We were aiming for a downstairs flat. So we went to a flat nearby, knowing now we were going to have a child. We got our downstairs flat in this house but we had to sign an agreement there. There were 13 clauses in that agreement and we signed the agreement to stay there for three years. We were paying 30 shillings a week there."

"Robert had come to the conclusion that he didn't want to get on any further. He was a station sergeant. He had no desire to get on any further. But I had been reading a book about Lloyd George (a Welsh Prime-Minister of Britain) during that time. I picked one up somewhere. Lloyd George had said that the marriage was the beginning of getting on. So I was most annoyed to feel that I was marrying a man who was quite willing to settle down with me, with children. Knowing him, he didn't want a lot of children. I said, 'Don't be so silly.' It was my encouragement to him that got him on the move again. In fact he was ill in bed, and he said 'If any man calls, well I'm ill in

bed.' *Actually he had the flu, and the flu was pretty grim in those days. The man that did call was really asking Robert to sign an application form for an examination. Well, I said, 'Put 'yes' on it.' I said, 'He's very poorly this afternoon. You can't see him, but you can go back and say 'Yes'. I'm sure he will do it, when he comes into the office.' Robert was horrified when he found out. There was a message now for him to go for the exam, because he had applied for it! The caller had been the Inspector of the station."*

"So now he had to go up. He came back and he was ever so pleased. He'd passed from Station Sergeant now to Inspector. Very shortly after that we had to leave to go now to Hackney."

The Metropolitan Police required that the newly promoted were relocated so that they would not have to manage their prior colleagues. It was a rational system but it did mean that the upward moving person moved often – as Robert did from Kilburn to Hampstead to Hackney to Hammersmith to Leytonstone to Staines to Fulham to Wandsworth and points in-between. A successful police officer inevitably got to know most of London during his rise.

"I immediately thought Hackney was the East End, said Edna." "We were going to the East End . . . oh, we didn't like it at all. We didn't like the thought of going from Hampstead to Hackney, but in Hampstead we had never made friends, and we wanted desperately to leave our flat. This was because the landlady of the house, in which we had a flat, lived upstairs. She was nothing short of a mad-woman."

"The baby now had been born, and but for the doctor, she then would have turned us out. She was a crank: a real crank. There were two attempts

123

on Jean's life, and one on mine. She got me right down. Helping her one-day, out of the lavatory, I thought she was in pain; she was whining and moaning. Robert was on night duty and I went upstairs to help her. I put her arm over my shoulder to help her up three steps to go to her bedroom, and she got hold of my neck and pulled me down. My gosh-alive, Robert woke up in a room underneath, hearing a terrific thud. I hadn't even come to when Robert came up and carried me down on his shoulder. That was the first time that he said 'You must never go, no matter what happens, never go into her flat.' She got out of it that way (because I was in her flat). I said, 'You'll feel better when I open the window', but she wouldn't let me go and open the curtains. She had all black curtains, with black coverlets on the bed . . . it seemed that a man had left her, and consorted with his maid, and had two children in the house."

"We were very desirous by this time to get out, and before the three years. But now we were held and she wouldn't release us. An agreement through a solicitor is binding, isn't it? She wouldn't release us, although she wanted to get rid of the baby."

"She had got at Jean, but I happened to be there and stopped her. 'Only just two little twists like that with your finger, and it will take years of worry and trouble away. Just two little . . . ' I said, 'Don't you dare touch my child.' I pulled the child away. Pulled the pram away. She (Jean) was in the pram, and the woman had come down now to my (flat). But there was no witness to prove that she had done it. She was very artful. She was a mad woman."

"Robert said 'There's only one way . . . ' There was only one clause, which safeguarded the tenants' interest. It was that, although the landlady had the right to all these twelve other clauses, the tenant had one sole right . . . 'To be left in peace.'

So Robert did all kinds of little things. And she screamed, she made noises and did everything. She was really dreadful to us, so on that clause alone we were able to leave. We went to Hackney."

"I was sure I was going to the very worst part of London. But funnily enough, though we twice lived in Cricklewood and Hampstead, off West End Lane it was, we never really found the neighbourliness we found in Hackney. When I went to Hackney, I was shown a flat there, again a downstairs flat, but a semi-basement. Our bedrooms were just down from the street in that type of house where you go up six steps to the front door. This was in Castlin Road, Hackney. When Robert showed me the house where we were going to go, I said, 'No, I wouldn't live here for all the money in the world, unless every bit of the paper was stripped off and it was lime washed.' It was all old dark dark paper. I said, 'Underneath this paper there must be no end of vermin.' It had been years and years on. I said 'It must be lime-washed', and you know, the landlord did it! He did everything and he limewashed the whole walls. Well, anyway it was quite clean in the end."

So Edna managed to apply a country solution, perhaps from her days on the farm where all the out-houses were lime-washed, to cleaning a London flat. Even though the Metropolitan Police Force had determined that they would live in Hackney, and on this occasion, found their home, she was still showing some signs of independence!

"In order to get coal in that house they dumped it underneath those front stairs, the coal dribbled in and you had an awful lot of dust. That got on the paper, so now I kept washing round the one portion till there was no lime left. Well eventually

125

it must have washed off. I don't know what happened afterwards."

"I must tell you a little bit about this flat. It had three rooms downstairs, and there was an old washing boiler, which I had never lit in my life, at the back. Now I thought, 'I must boil everything.' Not that we had ever done it for all the clothes even though we used a boiler at home. I knew you had to light a fire and put water in the boiler and boil the clothes. I was busy doing this one day and the other tenant from upstairs came down and she said . . . she was a real London girl, a cockney girl . . . she said 'Ee Luvey', she said 'Ee Luvey, let me do it. I'll put a fire underneath there.' So she lit the fire. Not only lit it, but she boiled the clothes, and she said 'You go and take that little girl outside in the garden.' She not only did that but she got to washing all these clothes. I hadn't even got the proper tubs. She washed the clothes and she said 'Hang them out, dearie. Keep that little girl out in the sunshine.' I had found a really good hearted woman."

Of course, there were no washing machines or dryers. Each home had a washday, which was ENTIRELY devoted to getting clothes clean. It would start early because the fire had to be lit and the first boiler-full of water had to be boiled with its load of clothes. After boiling and turning with a stick (usually a white water-worn broom handle) these clothes would be pulled out through clouds of steam and dumped into a large tub of cold water for rinsing. Then, while the next boiler full was started, these clothes would be mixed and moved about in perhaps three of four rinses of cold water, each tub taking considerable strength to empty and time to refill. After rinsing the clothes would be twisted to get out most of the water and then they would be hand mangled, and the load of still very damp clothes would be taken out to hang on the line outside. It was a day of toil (wet sheets in particular are very heavy and hard to manipulate) as several boiler loads would be on the go sequentially. When there wasn't loading there was rinsing to do, and when there wasn't rinsing there was mangling or hanging out. It might even all have to be repeated if it rained. Later there would be taking down from the line, folding and sorting. Those that went into the ironing basket would take that night or perhaps tomorrow to iron, with an iron heated at the fire-grate, before finally being restored to cupboard and drawer for next week's cycle. Of course if there were children, there might later have to be several other washes during the week (napkins were prime candidates for the boiler.) Sometimes it seemed that the kitchen or even the whole house was never free of steam and the smell of wet clothes.

"Also while Jean and I were playing out in the yard, the lady and gentleman from next door . . . Mr. and Mrs. Brown . . . were there. He was a man from Fleet Street, standing on his feet all day. He was getting old and his feet were bad. One day I met him and talked to him. He said 'My feet are bad. I can't stand.' He came in and I asked why didn't he put his feet in water while he is sitting by the fire? So that's what he did. Then she started playing with Jean. We got good friends there, real good, nice people. They also were Londoners. So now, instead of meeting the la-di-da people of Hampstead, who are mostly more or less Jews or very reserved English people, I met now the more

humble sort. Even in the market . . . Hackney Wick
market . . . even in the market there."

"*I was very happy in Cricklewood (Hackney).*
This upstairs lady, Mrs. Sogi, went down to Hack-
ney Wick and got a shop. It was a very little old
shop, you know, in Hackney Wick . . . selling gro-
ceries it was, you know . . . She invited us there to
tea, and when we got there, we went through this
little shop to the back. There was a nice white cloth
on the table, and in the middle of the table there
was a HUGE hank of bananas. Now he (the hus-
band) was a bargee, you see, and could get these
hanks."

"*Jean was with us. A little child's eyes are ev-*
erywhere, and she was looking at everything in the
shop. It was like a Christmas tree in a way: shiny
drums of biscuits, shiny this and shiny that. Ev-
erything was very nice, you know. Not very
tidy . . . a higgeldy-piggeldy shop it was. This lady
was delighted with the child, Jean. We were sitting
down around this hank . . . it was a HUGE thing,
you know. A big branch of bananas. She said 'Come
along,' she said. 'Ducky. Have a banana.' So Jean
stretched out. Now she had never been used to hav-
ing anything like that, so I dutifully got one ba-
nana off this blooming hank. It's hard to pull it
off a hank, you know. I got them, but they were not
ripe enough for me. Anyway, I squashed it and I
put a little bit of sugar and milk on it, and Jean
thoroughly enjoyed it. 'Have another, Dearie.' So I
said, 'Oh no, one's enough for her, thank you very
much. She'll have a bit of bread and butter.' Well
she went in the back somewhere and cut some bread
and butter and we had our tea that way. Now
after tea, the child had to go home. (Usually by six,
I'd start getting her ready and off she'd go to bed.)
Now 'Come on Luvey. Come to the shop. You shall
find out what you want.' So anyway, we went to
the shop and Jean chose the biggest box she could

see, which was a drum. She fixed it round her neck and we drummed our way home . . . it was quite a long walk . . . we drummed our way home, all the way to Castlin Road with this. Later I was horrified to find that it was . . . as big box of biscuits as big as a cake tin. The child could hardly walk with it. Well, she didn't know it was biscuits. So we drummed this thing all the way home, and she went upstairs to bed, still drumming it. Later we found out that this lady had lost two little children. Though when I had that tea, I realised why, if she'd been feeding them bananas at that age. (Laughing)."

Edna and Robert enjoyed a life of memorable episodes – good and bad — funny and not so.

"I'd asked Robert to take me to the seaside at Southend one day, and, there, I asked him to get some cockles, or mussels, or something. He got them on a little plate. I was disgusted with the little tiny plate that he got between two of us. In the market, I saw a barrow with the whole lot on. 'Well', I thought, 'I'll show Robert how to buy' even though I didn't even know what to ask for. 'How much'r you wanting, Missus,' he said, 'a pint?' I said 'Yes', not knowing anything. So he put a pint in a big bag, and off I went home. I thought 'I'll serve a meal out for Robert'. (Laughing) I went home . . . it happened to be dinnertime. I sprinkled pepper and vinegar on these winkles, and I said 'Come in, we've got a lovely dinner to-day.'"

"Robert looked at the table set for the winkles. There was a plate of winkles, a whole plate for him, and a plate for me, and a plate for the child. We were all just going to jolly well join in, and Jean had acquired the taste by having two, in Southend-on-Sea. Jean was about two and a half

to three then — only young. She didn't have a full plate, only had a small portion. However, Robert said 'I'm not going to eat this. I never eat shell-fish.' I don't know what meal Robert had instead, but you know, he never did (have shellfish), did he? But I had a plate, and Jean and I thoroughly enjoyed it. Robert was looking at us and smiling and laughing. He knew more about winkles than I did. We had a smashing meal. That evening, Jean went to bed and I said 'Well, we'll get this for you and I'm going to have the rest of the winkles.' So I sat down and ate the rest of the winkles. You can believe me or not, Robert laughed as he had never laughed in his life. I was groaning, and, ooh! I had a dreadful night. I vowed I'd never have a plate of winkles again . . . if I ever had a winkle it'd be off a little tiny plate like they have in Southend. I'd had too much. My gosh they can make you ill."

Like any other young married couple, Edna and Robert were very happy.

"I used to run to meet him. I think it was very much more on my side. He used to always be jolly when he came in and (I) ran to meet him, and the little girl ran to meet him. But the first thing he ever did when he came in the house was to stand by the first doorway and slip his trousers off, cause they were blue, you see. He wouldn't let Jean put a hand on his blue trousers. Oh No! Mustn't touch a policeman's trousers whatever you do. He had a name for being one of the tidiest men. No dirt on anything. No marks. No cotton or nothing. The first thing, hardly before he came in the house, was to slip his trousers off, and I used to get a pair ready for him to put on. And for a child to put a foot on his shoe was dreadful for Robert! Once we

got his trousers off, the child was able to crawl and do her hardest on him. He'd been once 'christened' when Jean was small, that's why. He shouldn't have been 'christened,' but he was."

"We were paying 30/-for that flat. There was no bathroom. But by this time we had a day bedroom for Robert, which is essential (for a policeman), and a night bedroom, and we also had a spare bedroom, where we could ask people. Robert's relatives came to visit us there. Aunty Mary came, and Aunty Martha, and Uncle Hartley, and of course my family all came to visit me while we were there. We had Victoria Park nearby; we only had to get out of the house and go to Victoria Park. But despite the situation, while we were there Robert was rather unhappy. He had met a man who had been working with him before."

"Previously, in another station, Robert had been of equal rank with this man. The other man didn't want Robert around and he reported, to the Superintendent that he had found Robert coming out of a Public House — drinking. Now, that's one thing Robert would never do. It so happened that Superintendent Hicks had been working with Robert and also with the other man. He knew the other man. So he listened to Robert, and he listened to the other man. He didn't move Robert, he moved the other man. But he moved him to Hammersmith, so now they had met again. Now, Robert saw a vacancy in Leytonstone in which we could have a house, or rather a flat above a police station. Superintendent Hicks was going to move so before he moved to Hammersmith, Robert asked for a transfer. He was transferred to Leytonstone as the Inspector there."

"We were very happy there."

"When you are living on the premises like that, all the grocers get to know you. Off and on during our married life, we would have gifts sent. Robert

131

would never take any gift, unless it went through
Scotland Yard. Sometime a gift would come to the
door for Mr. Graham with no address, no name or
anything, and he wouldn't even know where it was
from. Then he would ask his senior officer whether
he could accept it, and then he might accept it."

"Anyway, gifts started coming in. Like this:
there was a greengrocer across the way, and I'd
been used to phoning for my grocery order and I
would always say, 'Now don't forget, I want c-r-isp
eating apples.' So before I finished any
order . . . 'And any C-R-isp eating apples, Madam?'
he'd say. 'Yes, now don't forget, very good ones this
time.' Bit by bit, this man got to know that the wife
was doing it and she always wanted crisp eating
apples. Now there was never a week that I didn't
have a bag of these apples sent before I even sent
my order: crisp eating apples from the grocer across
the road. But these were not to Mr. Graham; they
were to Mrs. Graham. Well we got to know this
man. He was a Jew, one of the fine men, anyway.
In Leytonstone they soon got to know who's who.
In Sainsbury, we never dreamt of going to the
counter; the Manager would just run and serve
you. Well, I felt like a Queen. It was a smashing
place really, we were very happy. Jean by this time
was growing up and we'd take her to the shop.
One lady said 'Oh no, we won't have that suit for
her. Oh no, not the Inspector's little girl. We'll have
this one.' Although it was a little bit more in price,
they would know what would suit her. Oh, Jean
had a grand time between one and the other."

"When we bought our car, I'd had to take Jean
home to Towyn, so she wouldn't get scarlet fever
like Bertie in the upstairs flat above us. They used
to play together, and rather than get into contact
with scarlet fever, Robert and I took her down to
Towyn, and she was left there for nine weeks. When
I came back about three weeks after Maria, took

charge of Jean . . . I was calmly told (that) he'd bought a car!"

"I said 'Good Gracious me, where in the world . . . ' He bought his first car in Stratford. I said, 'How did you buy your car?' 'Well,' he said, 'I went to a shop and bought it.' They were then only shown how to use the thing, and he had to drive home from Stratford. I don't know (whether he had to have a license). I've no idea about that."

"I had to be taken down that night to see it, although I'd only arrived from Wales. We peeped at it in the garage."

"It was in one of these places where there were a lot of garages. So when you had to come out, you had to back your car out, bring it backwards. We came on to the road going up to Whipp's Cross. We had to go up there, and on a tramline."

"He'd arranged with a sergeant to teach him to drive properly, though he'd driven it away from the show-room all right. I didn't know anything, but anyway . . . he started first day in the morning and he came home in the afternoon. In the evening we had another chance to go with this car. I was allowed to come now with him."

"It was a car . . . oh, I wish I could remember the names of things . . . anyway, it was a car with a dickey seat: two in the front and a dickey seat in the back. (It was a Singer.) He said 'I'm not going to wait for Sergeant Halliard. Tut, tut, he's always late. He never could keep time.' He was very impatient, he was. Off Robert goes to the garage (with) me running behind him, you know. We got in the car and he reversed this thing out. He ran it straight out instead of running it out more like a curve past the tramway. Robert thought he knew what he was doing. Just going down that little steep hill there, I was sitting by his side, in the front seat with him. Terrified I was, but not as terrified as I might have been really. We see this Sergeant

*Halliard, who says 'It's all right, I'll jump on.'
And he jumps on the running board. We were just
going into the tramlines. While he was jumping
on, I was jumping out of the front seat for him to
get in by Robert. I got into the dickey seat in the
back, and Robert managed somehow or other to get
in front of a tram that was going by. The tram
driver was shouting like blazes at him, and it frightened the life out of me. I said, 'At the bottom of the
hill, don't forget to stop . . . I'm getting off.' They
did stop eventually at the bottom of the hill, and I
walked home. I had to walk home from Whipp's
Cross, ever such a long way. I walked home, but I
wasn't going to be driving like that. When he came
home, I said 'You silly. You (should) never start at
a car like that. You want to be cool, not do wrong
things like that. I knew that was wrong.' The way
he went in front of a tram that was coming down a
hill."*

Could Edna have learned to drive in Leytonstone
at the time of the first car, when she only had one
child, if she had wanted to?

*"Robert wouldn't let me. Robert wouldn't con-
sider it. No no, no no, Robert wouldn't consider it
at all, even though I said that he was getting the
best time at the wheel, and I wasn't. He said 'You
don't want to learn to drive.' You sort
of . . . because I hadn't earned . . . because it was
more . . . (because) it was natural for a woman to
depend on a husband, she depended on everything
he said. You see what I mean. You never thought
about it, but now . . . The first agitation I did
against all this was later when we went to Staines.
Now when the second child (John) was born in
Windsor, I came home and I was horrified to find
that our little Singer (car) had been sold. But we*

had a smashing new pram, you see. It was sold to a policeman, one of Robert's men, one of his detectives. As a reaction to that I wanted to learn to cycle. Robert still said 'No.' I'd seen a shop where you could hire cycles. I did (cycle at home). I had a friend there who had a cycle shop . . . Gwilym Arthur. I was very keen on going about, in a way, and I was much more keen on going about by myself, a little bit. I didn't want to be tagging along. Whenever I had to go out I had to go with Robert. I would go for long walks with the babies in the pram, and I used to love it. Well, anyway, I decided one day to hire a bike. The promise was that if I could cycle with a bike, I could have a bike. He had a bike, and Jean had a bike, but I didn't, you see. Now, I said 'I'm going to have a bike.' So, I did cycle. We cycled so far that Robert said 'We better turn back.' So eventually, when we turned back, he said 'Well, I'll tell you what. We'll try to go in for a car not a bike.' I was most disappointed then. There was no question of buying me anything, actually, you see."

The situation was clear " . . . it was natural for a woman to depend on everything the husband said . . ."There was no appeal court in those days, and the woman was so dependent that there was no thought of appealing anyway. She did of course try to circumvent the problem, though this didn't work for Edna either, even in this happiest of marriages.

But to get back to the new car in Leytonstone a few years earlier.

"Soon after that, Jean was coming back from Towyn (after her quarantine). Fair play to the family: one of the family drove up to London. It must have been Maria then. Maria had a car. She drove

her up to London, say on Friday, and we were going up (to the) North Country on the Saturday."

Robert's relatives all lived in Cumberland, about 300 miles to the North. In those days this was enough to make the location across the hills and moors quite remote. The brothers and sisters were proud of the young brother who had done so well, but they never did entirely accept his much younger wife, Edna. She was a Welsh stranger, and she remained outside the family. This was what the North Country meant to her. There was a single exception. Robert's eldest sister, Mary, had married a Cumberland boy and had emigrated to Canada—pioneering first in Alberta, where her husband became Mayor of Coleman, and later in Vancouver Island. Through her visits to Britain and thousands of letters, Robert's tie with Mary was strong. The two 'emigrants' understood each other better than did the Nenthead family. Later a similar understanding grew between Mary's daughter, Jean, and Robert's wife, Edna. They were of an age. It was a source of strength to both of them. However, for the moment, the North Country, symbolised a rather cold invitation.

Driving to the North of England was an expedition to be remembered – and then forgotten!

"This same sergeant Halliard said that he was going up to Scotland and he would lead Robert. Now he was going on a motorbike with two boys. Jean had traveled all the way from Wales in a motorcar, and we woke up three o'clock in the morning in order to be on the road before anyone else, and we got her sitting on my knee in the front. Now it shows how ignorant we can be: I never thought of saying 'We'll open the dickey seat and

let one of the boys, or even both of the boys, go in our seat.' But anyway, it was (probably) safer for us not to have helped anybody during the time!"

"Robert could go forward but he really couldn't reverse properly. When he started on that journey he'd never learnt to reverse properly. I was supposed to have been the navigator, and not knowing what to look for, I was always in trouble, all the way. Anyway, I'd say 'Where's he (Sergeant Halliard) gone? Where's he gone? I think he went over the bridge . . . right, over the bridge.' So we went over the bridge and we found that we'd gone the wrong way. We went along into some farmyard lane and Robert said 'Now then, blasted thing,' he said, looking at a gate. 'Dash it all, now what are we going to do?' He had to go through this gate and turn round because we couldn't reverse and turn back. So Robert just drove and pushed the gate down. I got out in temper, pushing Jean on the seat. There was only one door to this car, and you had to climb over it. Well, I went and pulled this gate aside for Daddy to turn round in the field and go back. (Then) we pushed the gate back. But the gate was down when we went through. He couldn't stop quick enough."

"Well, back over the bridge, and onto the main road, only to find Halliard had gone on ahead on the other road, and he (had) stopped and started making our breakfast. It was about nine o'clock in the morning. We had gone a long way out of London. Now he was busy making our breakfast and Robert caught him up. We were ever so happy. He told Halliard what he had done, but he didn't tell him held pushed the gate down. But I knew he had."

"I said to him, 'Now look here, we are not going to move until you learn to reverse.' So he said, 'Tut tut, don't be so silly. We've got a long

137

way to go. Now you get in the car.' So off we went in the car."

"You know how you go in the early morning . . . there was a milkman coming round, and Robert said as he was driving, 'That damn milkman's on the wrong side of the road.' 'Br-br-br-br' he honked, and he was shouting for this 'damned' milkman to get out of the road, and the milkman wouldn't go out of the road. Well, he said, 'if he doesn't go, I'll be over him.' 'Well,' I said, 'that's daft.' He braked so suddenly that Jean bumped her nose against the glass. The glass wasn't Triplex then, so Jean had a cut nose, and a cut upper lip. We didn't break the glass . . . but she must have bit her lip. It calmed Robert, and we went quieter after that . . . didn't sort of race."

"When we got to Scotch Corner, where the road to Scotland forks away, Sergeant Halliard left us then, just waving like that. We were on the road that Robert knew from his youth."

"Now we had to go over some mountains to Nenthead, and he showed me all these, and High Force (water-falls) and everything. He was on his own ground and by this time, I suppose, he must have been getting tired. We were calmly going along . . . he said, 'I know everywhere round here,' he said . . . We were going round at the same speed he'd been going on the better roads, in all these higgledy-piggledy lanes. All of a sudden we see a haycart coming towards us, and the man (was) really dozing as bad as the horse was. Poor old Robert couldn't stop, and the haycart couldn't . . . I don't know how we went past him, but we did. 'Daft idiot,' he said. It wasn't the haycart. The haycart had been used to going there, but it was Robert who should have stopped really, or reversed. Now that also pulled Daddy up a bit."

To undertake such a comparatively long journey

(250 miles) just after buying a first car seems an un-
wise idea, but only in retrospect. In 1928, driving
was an adventure rather than a calculated risk, so
three near misses were put down to experience!

*"A little bit later on, we stopped by the side of
the huge wall of a church. Now we had a meal and
a drink there on the side of the road. Mind, we
never went out without food. There were no vacuum
flasks or anything . . . if you wanted a hot drink
you had to make it on the roadside, somehow or
other. We had a pan and Primus stove. So we were
making this hot drink, a cup of tea, and Robert
said, 'Well, I'll try to reverse. Get in.' I said, 'No
we won't, we'll watch you.' I said, 'I'll clear up,
and we'll watch you reverse.' So he went along the
wall and he reversed. I said, 'Don't forget there's a
wall behind you.' So he reversed very very slowly.
You could reverse quicker, if you were not careful
with the clutch. You're giving the same pressure
then . . . it'll jump back. Well, he reversed once
and he just bumped a little bit, but not very much.
He'd learnt to go in reverse."*

*"We went halfway up the mountain now, to-
wards his home, in Cumberland. We got to a public house there. We thought we'd have a meal you
see. I forget the name of this place, but it's noted
for its cheeses. The cheese came there as a big round
cheese: a big big one. We were sitting there, and we
had had a meal. I think we had a little bit of time
to wait and we sat outside on a seat. While we
were there, one of these wayfarers . . . we would
now term them 'tramps' . . . he also came and sat
down on the seat. Now Robert had left home, let
me see, 14 years before. As we were sitting there
and watching Jean playing in front of us, this
wayfarer looked at Robert, and he said 'Eh, you're
not Jane Ann's son, are you? Are you Jane Ann's*

son, of Lunnon?' And our Robert was so pleased
that he was recognized as his Mother's son. You see
Robert was very fat actually then. In fact he was
17 and a half stone, and of course his Mother was
very stout. (Since I've got fat, he reckons I was like
his Mother! When he got thinner, he was more like
himself; you see (giggling)). Anyway, this wayfarer
recognized him as Jane Ann's son."

"The tramps there are men who go round selling sewing cottons . . . what would you call them?
Peddlers they were, Peddlers. They were always given
a meal, and he said 'No, not one of us were ever
turned from Jane Ann's door.' They were always
given food to eat and drink."

"Robert was ever so pleased. We were going
now in the car. We said good-bye to the tramp, and
shook hands, and Jane Ann's son had a wonderful send off that day in his car. Of course, the car
nearly went into part of a stone wall, this time. So
he realized that he couldn't wave and drive either
(laughing)."

"We were very careful now going along the
top of the mountains there. He pointed out to me
when we were there, all the whitewashed houses.
Every farm and every hamlet that you came to
nearby was all whitewashed. It was the cleanest
thing I'd ever seen."

"Then something happened . . . with the
brake."

"Robert didn't know anything about the in-
nards of cars at all, not one bit. But he says, 'Well,
I can hold it.' But we were facing now, down the
hill. We were going down the hill towards Nenthead,
a cross-country way. Well, we went down the hill
with Robert putting his foot, I suppose, on the brake
with his hand brake on. We were scared stiff. I was
scared stiff. Will it go? I was imagining us land-
ing down in the bottom . . . ooh! He was going to
hold it, you see. 'Well now, at the very bottom of

this hill,' he says, 'we've got a very sharp turning.'
'Well,' I said, 'stop before you get to it, and we'll
turn round ever so carefully by pushing the thing.'
We couldn't have pushed that car far because the
engine was very heavy, and our spare wheel was
on the side, and we even carried spare petrol too in
very special cans. We stopped on the bottom of that
hill and it was a sharper turning than we even
realized. It was a jolly good job we'd stopped, I
might tell you because we literally had to push this
blooming thing, step by step round. When you start
a car, 'specially if you're a new one at it, it goes too
quick, doesn't it? Good job he'd learnt to reverse a
bit, we did a three point turn to get round that
corner, though we didn't know what we were doing, and we went over a bridge, which didn't look
strong enough to hold us. Anyway, I walked over
it."

"Then we were over it and we didn't have to
go through Alston, we cut across then to
Nenthead . . . remember his home, where he had
lived, where he was born, in Lunnon, was the highest inhabited house in England. Then, they weren't
actually living as high as that, but even to go to
the house where they were living, in Whitehall, a
terrace of four cottages which he owned, was a very
large hill."

"He was ever so proud to come to see his people
there, with a car. It was a red car, I might tell you.
We were very posh in this car. But now we were
going up the last hill but one towards his Aunt's
house . . . They'd had a home nearby, and he
wanted to toot-toot properly in front of the Aunt's
house. He was disappointed . . . (sadly) the car
wouldn't go up the hill."

"So he had to stop it and then restart it. When
he stopped it, it was going backwards because the
brake wasn't holding it. I had to jump out somehow or other, over the dickey seat, while he held the

child, and I had to look for a stone. *You know when you're looking for a stone; you can't find one, can you? Well, eventually I got a stone which was too big for me to pull. Meanwhile the car had gone back so far so that it stopped on a level little bit, on its own! But anyway, we managed to get a stone eventually, and wedged it underneath, and we let the car rest a bit."*

"*I could see his house just above me from there. I said, 'I'm not coming in that car anymore. If you take that car it will go up the next hill without my weight and the child's.' And we walked up the hill past his Aunt's house and on to Whitehall. We arrived through the fields. He revved up . . . the last hill was a steep hill . . . he revved up the hills and he arrived in front of Whitehall. Meanwhile we'd got there before him and we saw him arriving. He arrived with such elation . . . tooting this . . . I think it was one of these things you knocked . . . and eventually we came in. 'Our Robert had arrived home with a car!'"*

"*It was 'Our Robert' this, and 'Our Robert' that from that time onward. I hardly understood them. That was my second visit to the North Country."*

"*His Father happened to be exactly the same in appearance as mine. I sort of took to the Father straight away because he was like my own Father, you see. He had a little sort of mustache . . . I suppose the same age, maybe a little older than Dadda . . . all their family were older. Yet his younger sister was only a year older than me. It was quite a visit, a real visit. (We stayed for) a fortnight: the fortnight the policemen had."*

"*That night when we went to bed, I had more kicks, I had more bruises on my body that night . . . he was kicking and braking all night long in bed. When we went down to breakfast next morning . . . I was one mass of bruises. I hadn't hurt myself except through Robert kicking. He was kicking me all night. He was braking the car all night long!"*

"Breakfast was one of these breakfasts, which was all starch, like pasties and butter: a North Country breakfast. Nothing very much, no bacon or nothing like that, like a Welsh breakfast! No, nothing, just pasties and butter and hot drinks. Anyway, it so happened that Lily was there, the younger sister. Lily was a dominating person in the way of her Father. She said 'Now Robert, now Robert, thou's got a car. Thou can take us to Newcastle. We're going to get a new piano.' I said then 'No, not likely, we're not going to no Newcastle to get a piano. If you felt like I do today . . . ' Anyway, Robert DID go to Newcastle during that visit, and he DID bring that piano back on his car. Just imagine' It was a ridiculous thing to do, and what's more, we broke some of the car in doing it. We had to have it repaired before we could even return to London. And you daren't be late for the Police . . . Robert wouldn't be late to his work. Anyway, during that time, I didn't even have a ride round the country that I meant to have."

The car journey to the North in 1928 was a huge adventure. Edna and Robert, and Jean, enjoyed themselves cooking and eating by the roadside, and overcoming a number of problems on the way there. Today, the same journey would take four or five hours without incident. Then, when the main occupants of the roads were still tramps and haycarts, the excursion was akin to a voyage into the backcountry today. Edna was first mate to the Captain, and there was no thought of equal participation . . . responsibilities were divided, but Robert took the larger decisions. Nevertheless, even though this might seem a

143

poor way to go in retrospect, at that time it was quite harmonious and understood. They were happy together.

Back home in London . . . they were both subject to the Metropolitan Police needs.

"From Leytonstone now he was moved to Staines. Every time he passed an examination, with promotion, (we had to move). He passed an examination and shortly after that his move came to Staines. We had nine days in which to move. Now we were adept at moving by this time. Remember we were not collectors of anything really, because we couldn't be. Every room was different. Even Jean by this time, was quite able. I said 'We've got to go and follow Daddy to Staines, you know.' The first thing she ever did was to stand on a chair to get the pictures down (laughing). That was the first thing we ever did. She'd roll these carpets up. . . . She'd be as quick as a needle. She'd be rolling these carpets, and within nine days we were down in Staines."

"All this time, Robert would travel by car, by police car from Leytonstone. In Staines, he was going as a Station Inspector."

"Lord Trenchard was called in (by the British Government) to clean up the Metropolitan police in general and he chose certain men to clean up selected areas. Robert was selected for Staines. But Robert was so surprised that, after his passing the examination, he was up for promotion so quickly. When he was chosen, he said, 'What do think.' he said, 'I'm going to Staines.' When he had been there one or two days Lord Trenchard himself came to see him. (Being above a certain rank, Robert was no longer Sergeant or Inspector, he was now plain 'Mr. Graham' . . .) 'Mr. Graham,' Lord Trenchard said, 'you've got full charge of here and

you can call on as many men as you like. I want it cleaned up.' There was a lot of corruption in there, in so much that there had been an Irish Station Inspector, a Roman Catholic man. This Inspector, who had gone into the . . . he was a Mason . . . he was consorting with publicans, you see, and being paid off."

"When Robert came to Staines, the head depot of Staines is Hammersmith, where he had to go for his money on the Wednesday. He had five stations reporting to Staines, which now take in part of the London aerodrome (now Heathrow). He had five inspectors, each in one of these outlying stations and he had forty or fifty men. It was a big station (in) a big area. Having a post like Staines, and an area around it, you're responsible for the whole area. The area went from Hammersmith to Staines, and then went to Egham Bridge. Then it went right down to Hampton Court, along the river. He had a big area there of the river and a lot of the country."

"He had two drivers allocated to him, one who lived in a flat opposite and one who lived in a little house by the side of the station. Robert found, very shortly, that the one who lived in the flat was a very decent fellow . . . a really decent trustworthy fellow, but the one who was living in the little house and had two children . . . He was giving instructions to Robert on where to go, what to do and what not to do. So Robert could see he was an evil influence. He had levy on the other driver as well . . . they were both together, you see. So he called him one day, and he said 'Well now look here, I want you to transfer yourself to . . . I want you to sign this form to ask for a transfer.' 'I'm not going, Sir.' 'Well, either you do that, or you'll be sent to the Headquarters, Scotland Yard.' 'I'm not going, Sir. I'm quite happy here. I've got my house and everything' 'You do as your told: you either sign

145

this now . . . ' That's how they did it you see. There was no question of choice. You either signed for a transfer, or you get sent up to Scotland Yard, and you'd be sacked. That's what it all meant really. So he signed for a transfer, and off he went. We never saw anything more of that man."

"The funny part of it all was that the Chief of Hammersmith was his old boss from Hackney; Hicks. Also there was the other man who had been transferred to Hammersmith, as an Inspector. Now, Robert was a Station Inspector; above this man, you see. He couldn't say anything . . ."

"When we were in Staines, Jean started school, so she was five or six. There I had my second child. (We went to a nursing home to have Jean) . . . and now in order not to be more private, we went to Windsor. It's only a motoring distance. We went to Windsor because there was a very good nursing home there. The Princess Margaret Nursing Home, I think it was. Also, by this time, we were living above the police station amongst a lot of men. While you're pregnant, you're not blatant during that period are you? You're rather reserved. So being away in Windsor was nice."

"Anyway, when the child was born, I think we both achieved our object in having a son. It's a son a north-countryman wants first. Although by this time Robert had accepted the daughter, who was about five and a half. I remember when the son was born . . . We had an open tourer car then, and we had just got Jean (quietly, remembering) better from whooping cough, and John was born. When I went back home from the nursing home. I was horrified to find that he'd sold the little car. But instead we'd got a smashing pram! A big one from the shop window, you know. You know how they show the best. One of these . . . oh, we had a smashing pram . . . But I still wanted the motor-

car, you see, didn't I? It takes a wife off her feet, besides the baby."

"John was born and Jean was six and a half. 13 months later we moved to our next home in Fulham. Robert was moved to the Walton Street station."

"Before his appointment to Walton Street station, we were on holiday. Robert was called back. The police were never given a reason why they were called back, but every policeman wonders what he has done wrong. They are really so regimented in a way that that all through their life as a policeman there is a sort of nervousness there, to do right, you see. Not to break the law . . . that's all it means. You could easily break a law by just doing one little wrong thing. Somebody could report you. Anyway, poor Robert went back to London . . . worried to death, he was . . . After he went back, he sent me a wire by return and he said 'All-right. Everything O.K.' He wasn't allowed to finish his holiday."

"I finished my holiday in a short time and then went back to London, only to find that Robert had had to go to Lord Trenchard again, now in Scotland Yard. He was very very pleased with the work he had done in Staines, and had recommended him for further promotion. So now a transfer first, with a bigger area around Walton Street, which took in Harrods, all round Victoria, all round the Buckingham Palace and the Royal quarters round there . . . it went ever such a far way out. But we had our house in Fulham then."

"Now Robert was one of two Station Inspectors. They were working under a Superintendent. They had a very very big area. They were there again to clean up that place. Lord Trenchard took him aside and told him the same as before: that he could call on anybody he liked, that now he was to be in — smash-and-grab! They went in more for

147

*smash-and-grab raiding then. He was mostly in
charge of that department, sort of thing . . . while
his colleague was to do a station inspector's work
more like what Daddy had been doing."*

"A little time after he had been there, he had to
go up again to Scotland Yard, and he was given
the promotion to Crime Chief. 'Crime Chief' today
would be a 'Chief Superintendent' today. As a Crime
Chief he couldn't live in police quarters. We now
were living outside, although in a house in which
there where two policemen—one a detective underneath us. Then a little later, for the first time in
our life we had a house in Wandsworth. Funnily
enough, we were living in the same road as his
Superintendent, so they met unbeknownst to anybody. He and his Superintendent worked very well
together."

"Now, his work was not so much in the details
of smash-and-grab as it had been. As the Crime
Chief he was in charge of the 'Prevention and Detec-
tion of Crime'. They found that the detectives and
the uniformed branch were not working together,
so this was an intermediary sort of force in between, to make them cooperate. If an uniformed
man found a burglar, he didn't want all the glory
to go to the detectives. And the detectives didn't
want to the opposite, so they sort of worked against
each other to a certain extent. Robert's job was also
to be a mediator, even between the criminal and
the force. Sometimes he was taken quite kindly and
other times he would be laughed at, because he was
in uniform."

"Wandsworth Prison was in our area, but he
had nothing to do with that, because his area was
actually Kensington. Around Kensington: that was
his big area. He had a wonderful job too, whereby
he looked at these criminals round Chelsea. This
was where all the immorality was going on, you
know the such-like thing. Although he knew of it,

*he had very little to do with it. Every Wednesday,
he had to go up to Scotland Yard to be taught more
about crime. It became more and more interesting.
This was about 1936."*

In speaking about HER life Edna actually speaks
about Robert's life. They were one and the same
things. She had now almost no independent life. She
cared for two children and looked after the home.
At Wandsworth for the first time they had a garden
and they kept a few chickens, harking back to their
country upbringing even in London. She looked after the garden too. There was absolutely no thought
that she might have her own life, her own job, or
really her own friends. Her acquaintances, apart from
her family and close neighbours, were his. This is
not to say that Edna missed anything. She and Robert had a successful and happy life, and she was content with his successes. It may today seem strange to
us, but in the late thirties it was the norm. In 1928
women in Britain had gained the right to vote, but
apart from a small band of political activists, this still
meant little to the majority of women. Certainly Edna
missed nothing in living closely with her husband's
successes.

*"Now by 1937, there was all this scare about
war. Before Robert was due to be retired, he was
made the liaison officer between the evacuees of
London and the police. They had already gone as
far as arranging that he had to live in the police
station, and his bedroom was made there. He
wouldn't even be allowed home. So Robert's anxi-
ety was to get us out of London, before war was
declared. He asked me if I'd go to Canada. Knowing his people, I said 'No.' but I'm sorry in a way*

149

that I didn't. My children might have been Cana-dian!"

"During that time because of his retirement, we were looking for a house on the south coast. We had decided on a house, and were nearly in the final stages of buying a house in Angmerin-on-Sea: Angmerin near Worthing. This house would have been built, ten or twelve years before. But it could be made beautiful. There was a stream at the bottom of the garden, and the sea not very far off. It was rather of the Old World. It was a de-tached house, and we were looking forward to it. A two-storied house, it was, you know, and it was rather big: bigger than the one we've ended with in Wales. Angmerin was quite a small place. But the Angmerin area and the south coast of England came in the area from which Robert was to evacu-ate all the children. So he said then, 'Now look here now. I'm not going to evacuate my children to the south coast. I'm going to get mine somewhere else. That's the area they are going to bomb.' And so they did. So Robert squashed the purchase and we looked elsewhere."

"It so happened there was an indecision in our/my mind (in between us, you see), on whether Robert would retire when his time came, or whether he wouldn't, or whether he shouldn't. He happened to be in the last batch that was even allowed to retire. He was lucky in a way to get out and to take us away."

"During the summer holidays before we had seen the house we are living in now, in North Wales, in Pwllheli, North Wales. We had tried to buy it, but they wouldn't sell it, they would only let it. But now we received an offer by mail and this tipped the scales. Robert decided to retire and go to the house in Wales that was now offered to us for 100 pounds less than we had bid for it the year before! He read that letter in Paddington, when he was

putting us on the train to get us out of London. That was £1,100, and we had offered £1,200 for it."

"We, the children and I, went off to Wales, Robert saying to me as he was leaving me . . . 'I'll buy that house even if we don't live in it. It's a good buy.' He had been through a war before, and he had NOT bought houses when they were offered to him before. So he vowed now that he wasn't going to lose this opportunity. There was another war coming and he thought 'I'll buy it whether I live in it or not.'"

"Robert had always wanted to go to Towyn. The Towyn house was vacant, and I had evacuated with the two children to Towyn first. But I didn't stay in my old home. I went to digs there. I did go down and I wanted to get the key. I also wanted permission from the executors of Dadda's estate to go there. One of the executors said 'Yes, by all means, get in the house. You go and take the house, if you've got to evacuate from London, then go by all means.' That was Uncle Llew, but meanwhile Aunty Gretta put her spoke in it . . . not saying 'No', but instead invited us up to Chwilog to come and stay with her. When I arrived at Chwilog I found that she was in an old manse there, with no lamps . . . only oil lanterns . . . no conveniences at all, no water (you had to carry water) . . . no toilet conveniences or anything. I was getting fed up of all this and I thought 'If we are going to live in this area it won't be here.' I was so upset living there that I thought I'd get into digs in Pwllheli where John and Jean could go to school. Meanwhile I wrote to Robert."

"So I got into digs in Pwllheli. Nobody would take me first because I was evacuated with two children. You couldn't get into anywhere at the beach, you couldn't get . . . I tried Salem Terrace, and no end of places. Nobody would take you in.

*It was also the end of the year when everybody had
finished taking anybody in."*

Pwllheli was also a resort town, much like Towyn,
although since it was also the market town for the
Lleyn Peninsula, it was slightly larger. The towns-
people took in English visitors and early in the war
they had difficulty in distinguishing evacuees from
visitors. Since the season was over . . .

*"Eventually anyway I managed to get into
King's Head Street. That's where I stayed with the
two children. I was also near the school where I
could see if they ever started in school. I was only
going to stay there until Robert decided to retire.
His retirement came in less than a month."*

Chapter 8

Snapshots

The album is a small black bound book with dark grey pasteboard paces. The fly-leaf is inscribed 'With fondest love, June 3rd, 1925, Robert.' On each page, held in small cutouts, there are four photographs.

The photographs used to be black-and-white, but now they have mellowed. Shades of brown and ochre have taken away the harshness of the summer sun and the shadows of those days, fifty years ago. The photographs have frozen the times. Each instant is preserved within the boundaries of the small squares of paper, until eventually it fades with other memories.

The inscriptions below the prints are faded now. Just enough remains to locate the place and year.

153

In June, Robert was courting Edna. He took her to Sandy Lodge and they sat on the grass to eat their picnic. It was hot, and Robert took off his coat. The photograph shows him in his shirtsleeves held up by armbands. He is offering a bottle of soft drink. Edna, in the next photo is wearing a dark coloured silky dress in the plain fashion of the day, with her hat on the grass beside her. She looks, with a faint smile, a little embarrassed by his attention.

Later that same month, there was the most important visit to the British Exhibition of Wembley, where Robert was to meet Edna's mother and father for the first time. He charmed them. The fading print shows Robert alone. He is dressed very formally in a white shirt, grey tie and a dark suit: top button fastened, and a silk kerchief in his top pocket. He must have had difficulty dressing to meet his prospective parents in-law and, at the same time, to be comfortable for a summer day walking around a trade exhibition. He had chosen formality, for his dark suit was topped off with a black bowler hat. Yet, even out of uniform he was still a policeman. He stood erect in front of an enormous ornate stone Chinese lion, with his hands clasped behind his back; clearly a London copper standing on the street corner. He seems about to say 'Now, what's all this 'ere about?'

Edna appears on the next page sandwiched between her Mother and Father. They are seated on a bench beneath the statue of a Gladiator who will be forever cut-off at the knees.

Edna's parents were 61 and 63. Her Mother, Jane, sat unsmiling for the photograph looking away at something in the distance. She was an imposing woman, comfortably stout with a firm face. She looked as though she could have been a devil to get around if she had taken a dislike to you. Fortunately for Robert, she didn't. On this day out she wore a smart suit with the coat opening to show a pleated blouse covering her ample bosom. She liked bright things, so she wore a brooch on her blouse, and her large hat was decorated with a feather and a bunch of coloured flowers. Edna's Father, Thomas, even though he wasn't smiling either, looked kindly. It was the white mustache that did it; it bushed across his upper lip framing his mouth in a permanent friend-liness. He was on vacation in London from rural Wales so he too wore a best suit and bowler, but his hooked walking stick looked more Welsh than Wembley.

Edna had worn a light dress coat that morning. It had wide silky embroidered lapels to the waist show-ing a plain white blouse buttoned at the neck. Her cloche hat had a large forward brim to protect her face from the June sun; its broad ribbon matched her dress. Her smile showed that this was HER day. Those she loved surrounded her.

Later that year, in August, Edna and Robert went on a day's outing to Brighton on the south coast. She wore a plain chequered half-sleeved frock with white collar and cuffs and a small dark bow at her throat. A frivolous white hat topped the outfit. Her sensible shoes were fastened with a strap across the instep . . . pure 1925. She sat on the rowing boats on the beach and leaned on the railings of the Brighton Pier for her photographs as the wind fluttered her dress against her stockinged legs. She was 24. Rob-ert was 35. He was tall and well built as befitted a policeman, and even on this day out he wore a dark suit, tie, silk handkerchief in his top pocket, and — a black bowler. But as he sat on rowing boat, his broad smile would have charmed any young girl. It had certainly captured Edna.

Back in London, Robert usually wore uniform. He wore it well. Everything was in place; the chain holding his whistle looping beneath his tunic, the striped cuff of the London Police, and shoes shining bright black. The crown above the stripes showed his rank of Station Sergeant on his arm. His station number, S.120, shone at his tunic collar.

One last photograph from 1925 shows the end of an era. In a courtyard of a large brick-built institutional building, which the caption shows is 'St. Peter's Hospital, London, September 1925', stands Edna in nurse's uniform. Her chosen profession had her in white: in a sparkling starched white bib over a white dress. Her curly hair is tucked into a white cap barely hanging on her head. This was the end of her nursing career. She was married a month later.

Jean was born in 1926 and from then on family photographs invariably included children.

Robert was earning enough that they could take vacations, so the tradition of a summer vacation, a week at the seaside, became firmly fixed. Today everyone expects to 'go away' for a summer holiday. In the late twenties, the idea was just beginning, but the car enabled anyone with the time to reach the sea. There is nowhere in Britain further than 60 miles from some piece of the coast, and it was to Little Hampton, Sheringham, Worthing, Brighton, or even Colwyn Bay in North Wales, that Robert took the family.

The photographs showed children building sandcastles, standing by finished sandcastles, and sometimes even buried in sandcastles. Jean first, and later John, showed off their prowess. Then there were photographs showing groups. English beaches are usually windy, and invariably Edna would be forced to search behind wind-breaks and day tents or beach huts to find the children for the mandatory record of attendance, the group photograph.

Fashions of the day appeared in a 1931 photograph at Frensham Ponds in Surrey. Seated on the running board of an open touring car sat Robert, with his daughter Jean beside him. They wore identical bathing outfits: one piece, with shoulder straps holding up a woolen costume decorated in broad horizontal stripes of colour. Robert's had just the barest semblance of legs, but Jean's had no skirt. Fashions had changed and these costumes were daringly mdern.

In 1932, the vacation was to the North of England to 'Scotch Corner', Dykeheads and Nenthead. Jean was allowed to run around the farmyards, playing with the farm dogs and helping to make hay with the Graham family. The hay was cut by scythe in the hill fields, then raked and gathered by hand and loaded onto a cart to take it to the barn. Everyone worked. Soon after breakfast everyone would follow Granddad to the fields. Some of the men would carry the scythes and their sharpening stones, while the women would bring the broad wooden rakes. The scythes, and the sickles used close to the stone walls, were dangerous and it was rare that any of the men escaped some permanent scar. Robert carried a scar on his right hand where he had cut nerves so badly that he could never hold a pen between thumb and first finger. He wrote a fine flowing script holding his pen between the first two fingers. So the men used the scythes, and the women worked behind them raking the hay into long lines first, for drying,

157

and then later into piles for collection. The children jumped in the hay and chased the rabbits as they ran from cover. At midday some of the women would fetch food: bread, cheese, perhaps some meat, and buttermilk freshly cold from the churn that was kept in the cool shadows of the stone byre. If there were storm clouds about then eating would be cut as quickly short as possible to save the hay before rain came, but if the weather was good, then midday was a picnic. Everyone enjoyed it, despite the tiredness that was beginning to creep into the shoulders from wielding the scythes and rakes. The afternoon would stretch out as everyone tired. The palms of the hands became sore from the constant rub of the rake handle, and little pieces of hay would start to itch where they had got inside the clothing. So at the end of the day, just before the light was finished, everyone was glad to stop. Yet, walking alongside the cart, holding Jean on the broad back of the horse, Edna felt that something good had come of the day. It had been worth it.

The photographs showed that Robert's father had an almost identical white bushy mustache as Edna's father. But for his flat cloth cap instead of her Father's black bowler, they were identical. It was no wonder that she said

> *'I sort of took to his Father straight away because he was like my own Father, you see. He had a little sort of mustache . . . I suppose the same age, maybe a little older than Dadda . . . '*

After 1933, family photographs included John.

John's pram, which was awaiting Edna's return from hospital with her new baby, is shown in several photographs. It was her pride and joy . . . today it looks an antique . . . The family is caught by an unknown camera, walking around a corner in Colwyn Bay, in North Wales. Robert has abandoned his suit and bowler for a practical family man's raincoat and umbrella. Still it is summertime as his open collar shows. Edna too has a raincoat; open over her spotted dress with white bib. She pushes the pram. John is leaning over the front, like a smiling mischievous figurehead of a sailing ship. Jean, in school-uniformed beret, blazer and shorts with a white shirt, holds onto the pram handle. The family is complete.

These photographs, dated between 1932 and 1937, show that Edna put on weight. Her activities were confined to the home and family, and Robert had not even allowed a bicycle. It was inevitable that the pounds would accumulate: from a slim nurse in 1925, to an attractive mature woman of 1931, to slightly overweight wife of 1935, to 'comfortably' fat in 1937. In those days, Edna would avoid being in the front of photographs.

Like all other wives, mothers of two growing children, Edna was never idle. In Staines, Jean was doing well in school; there were costumes for school plays and dresses for parties to be made, concerts to be attended and a new child on the way. In Wandsworth, Edna and Robert had a house for the first time, so they kept chickens in a wire-netted run in the back garden. John is shown in one photograph wearing knitted jersey and trousers, feeding two brown hens and a large white cockerel.

A picture of the new car in Wandsworth catches John. It was an open yellow tourer, with running board complete with an outside fuel can. It was almost a miniature of Robert's first car, the Clino. The car is

159

askew the garden path and John is waving at the photographer.

> *"My hair blew in the wind as the car, my alter-ego, and I, tore down the hill. I gripped the wheel and crouched as pedestrians scattered. Then the corner was upon me . . . there was absolutely no way to turn around it at this speed . . . and yet, to avoid the drop beyond . . . I tried anyway. As the front wheels turned to hold a new line, the momentum threw the car up and over. It spilled me on the roadway and came to rest on its side across the path with its upper wheels still turning. My leg was torn at the knee."*

It was one of John's earliest memories, but the crash came in his own pedal car. It was metal painted a quick red and he had been coming down the pavement hill far too fast to turn the right-angled bend into his home street – Tylehurst Road, Wandsworth.

Robert, like any working husband of the time, had his own separate life among his working colleagues, the police. He supported the police tug'o'war team. He sits in the front row of a group of hefty athletes. In front of the team lie their shield and cup trophies and their rope: a two-inch diameter hemp monster. None looked as if they would have much difficulty in keeping the peace on their beats!

As ranking officer, Robert also appeared formally in other group photographs . . . here he sits alongside a table-full of silver cups above an immense silver shield. Superintendent Honour, Chief Inspector Graham and Inspector Butcher are immortalized in chairs placed above a tiger skin complete with snarling head. Yet the real personalities of the photograph were the four skinny police constables in the background, clad in athletic shirts and shorts: their bony knees just visible through the table legs. They were the Barking-to-Southend Championship long distance running team of 1938!

Edna had no part in these activities. She went, once a year, to the Divisional Christmas Ball but there was very little other involvement with the police once the family was growing. However since she had lived above the police station in Staines and was recognized in her neighbourhood as the Inspector's or Chief Inspector's wife, she felt that she belonged to the police almost as much as Robert did. When he retired from the police in 1939, she retired at the same time. Later, after Robert's death in 1964, she even joined and became active in the National Association of Retired Police Officers (NARPO).

Chapter 9

Retirement and the War

'*When he retired we were jolly glad to find now, that Robert had bought this house by giving a deposit of 100 pounds. That's what he gave for 'Wal-Cum'.*"

The house became 'Wal-Cum' from the first three letters of Edna and Robert's respective homes, Wales and Cumberland. However for the next thirty-four years the name was habitually mispronounced by all and sundry, as 'Welcome' — a happy and appropriate mistake.

> "*We were allowed to go and see it, but not to go in it until all the final papers were done. So I used to take the children up the mile hill everyday past that house and we used to walk back . . . 'One*

day, perhaps we'll live in that house.' We never even stood at the gate. I only just said one day 'We'll do it.' By this time, the youngest, John was beginning to miss his Father. He was allowed to climb over every stile we came to, and he rebelled against walking. He didn't like the walking. He was four and a half. He suddenly said to me 'Are we going to live like this always?' 'No,' I said, 'Daddy's going to come back.' He had got used to having a car. Because he'd been taken on a Sunday morning to Walton Street police station (in London) to play with the flags and sit on the police horses, while Robert did part of his work.

Anyway, in 1938, Daddy arrived in Wales with a little Ford car. A 'Ford 8' car it was (with the number ATM 250.) We'd had a car in Staines, a Singer, our open tourer. Then we had this Ford 8. We only paid £30 for it, and it was in smashing condition. We never went near the garage to get anything done. When he arrived, we were jolly glad to see Daddy and the car. The car played a big a part then because we could move. Robert stayed one night in King's Head Street, and then we went up to the house. It happened that we went into the house on the anniversary of the date when he had joined the police."

"We went there, and he said 'There you are, there it is. While I'm alive, here's your house. And here's the money whereby you can live.' He gave me his cheque from the police for a month. 'But always remember,' he said, 'it's a month in advance.' (Laughing). 'There it is, pick it up,' he said. 'There's your house.'"

"He sent the children out into the front garden, and he properly gave me the house. He gave me a kiss. He handed me the cheque, the 'money to live'."

Robert had bought the house in Edna's name,

given outright as a gift. This retirement was to be a joint one rather than just another step in his career. It shows a remarkable strength, in those days, for a man who had always been used to ordering people about to contemplate retirement (after 26 years in the Police), at only 49. He was leaving the city for the country and at the same time making his wife a more than equal partner. It was probably not a conscious decision, simply an act in which there was no doubt of their unity.

> *"He said then to me. 'I've even got clogs . . . for the garden'. There was no garden as such; it was just an undug piece of land. I said, 'Well, I'll have my dream'. I always had in my mind that MY strong man was going to be a man like a cowboy. He had to have heavy boots on and make a noise. So we were laughing, and just then the children returned, and we went to look at the house. I stood in every window, and said 'We don't even need curtains here with nobody overlooking at us.' The picture from every window was beautiful. After coming from London, it was heaven, wasn't it?"*

The house, 'Wal-Cum', stood on the crest of a ridge overlooking the sea. Just below, the beaches at Abererch were about 300 feet down and a mile away across a patchwork of stone-bordered fields. Cardigan Bay stretched from Criccieth Castle and the Black Rock on the left, around to Pwllheli's Gimlet Rock on the right, with broad sandy beaches between. In the distance across the bay, twenty miles away, were the blue misty Cambrian hills of Meirionyddshire, ranging from Snowdon (the highest point in England and Wales) itself on the left, to the Irish Sea on the right. In the center was Cader ldris above Edna's old home of Towyn. Directly opposite on the far bay coast stood the majestic 13th Century Harlech Castle, famed for the 'Men of Harlech'. The view took your breath away the first time you saw it. The house was designed for the scene since every main room faced forward with the same view. Visitors would stand entranced on the front lawns. But at this moment, there were no lawns and there was no garden; there was just a downhill swathe of field.

"Robert retired exactly (after) 26 years (of service), an extra year beyond the requirements to get a pension of two-thirds of his wages. If he had retired at 25 years, he would have had only half. The police force was hard and many men were cast out at 25 (years). They were harder in a way to their own men, and the wives meant nothing. A wife of a policeman meant nothing. Anyway, he retired."

"War wasn't actually declared, when we retired in October 1938 though it seemed inevitable. When Chamberlin went over to Munich (and returned with 'Peace in Our Time' after meeting with Hitler); that is when we retired."

The unity of Edna and Robert, and Edna's assumption of Robert's career as her own, are very clear. Robert didn't retire, 'WE retired.'

"Meanwhile, before war was declared, we were very proud of our 'buy', but one part, in the front of the garden, by the gate, was all fenced off. Robert warned me to keep the children off that part behind that fence. They did keep off because they were used to (prohibited areas) in London. It seemed that the lady, Miss Maudsley, who had sold us the

165

house, sent the plan, accepted the 100 pounds, and really and truly, she could not, should not, have sold it. She also sold the land on which the house stood which belonged to her Mother, Mrs. Maudsley. When Mrs. Maudsley found that her daughter had sold the house AND the land, and sent all the information about it to Robert, she was refusing to sell her land. We were in a bit of a pickle, because we had nowhere else to go. They even offered us 70 pounds to get it back. But we had paid 100, and we had paid for the transfer from London; the first move we had paid for. Anyway, she had done wrong, so eventually her solicitor explained to her and eventually it was settled. We even got the last piece of land, and she never made any fuss about it. Now we were our own full owners. We knew we were in a safe area for the children."

"The first thing that Daddy thought of was an air-raid shelter for his children. He started digging like anything. He dug by the gate, and he came across a whole stratum of rock going right through it. He wasn't allowed to blast (and use dynamite), he knew the law too well. He could have done a little bit of blasting, I think, but if you're within a certain area of houses you can't blast. He dug it by hand, putting a big crowbar into a crevice in the rock to break it up. He edged the crowbar in and he would hammer and hammer until he cracked the rock. We were ever so pleased with this. The children, John and Jean, saw all this done. We looked on, it was wonderful. Robert had had mining experience, a little bit. He knew more about stone than we did, but everybody around the area was so surprised that he was doing all this by hand. The air-raid shelter was eventually built, after many weeks. A lot of work that was — to build. We had 12 cartloads of stone. He knew where he was going to put that air-raid shelter from the first day. He *knew it was going to be under two trees between the house and the road. We worked ever so hard until he got the air-raid shelter done."*

"When this air-raid shelter was built, war was declared. He gave me instructions: if he ever had to leave me, what to do. He told me what to do in the event of an attack."

Then came the garden . . .

" . . . we dug and we dug and we dug. I was even saddled (harnessed) onto the barrow. He pushed and I pulled. I was getting a good weight and thoroughly enjoyed it. The children would push too, and we'd sift all the soil. We made a garden like that."

Robert was carefully securing his family's future.

"He'd got a roof over my head. His original intention, when we first got married, was to get me two houses: one whereby I could get a rent to live from, and one to have a roof above my head. He always had that idea. He never meant to get a big family, but he was very pleased eventually when he got his son and daughter."

"He always used to take me outside of the house in order to tell me these things. You know, the old proverb about 'walls have ears', and all the rest of it. We'd go and sit down on the old garden seat he made by the air-raid shelter, after the children had gone to bed. It was not only a rock we had to contend with, we had to contend with a tree, which had fallen and embedded itself into the earth. He had to dig round this big tree that had fallen. The land had been a chicken run for Jones Ysgol-dy before the outside wall had been built, so it was all

167

overgrown. Eventually he worked very hard and out of the branches of this tree he made that seat."

"I remember how we cut the logs at night. John and Jean would be indoors. Jean would have instructions to call me when it was seven o'clock. I'd be out helping him. We worked together like anything."

"During that time, I wanted chickens. I felt sure that chickens would be very useful. We had found a house there, on the way to Caernarvon, where you could buy a chicken for boiling. A boiling chicken was half-a-crown then. So coming from a large family and being economical, I said 'Well we better buy two.' We brought them home and put them under a box. Oh no, they weren't dead, live chickens they were and we had to kill them and everything. Live chickens. Next morning they were chuckling and chuckling and chuckling like anything. So my Gracious me, we found an egg! So we kept the two for a time because we didn't know which was laying. Well, Robert soon found out and he chopped the head off the other one . . . or rather, he killed it. He used to kill a chicken with just knick on the back (of the neck) with his thumb. That was the beginning of our farmyard. We kept that hen until she stopped laying."

"Meanwhile Easter came along and I was buying Easter eggs for the children. Jean said, 'I don't want a chocolate Easter egg, I want a real one.' So I, being Welsh, went to the boy of Llwyn'rhudol farm, asked him if he had a hen or any little chickens. So he brought me a late hatch. It was the best thing I ever did. We paid 7/6 for this late hatch: thirteen chickens PLUS the use of the hen. By this time Robert had dug the bottom of the garden, and he'd done all his fences all right. That was one of the first things he did in that garden, was to make the fences all right . . . our property, you see. We'd got a black currant bush or

two, and we had a wire netting over these black
currents. Anyway the chicks went in there in a box.
Robert said, 'I don't know how you expect me to
make a garden and have hens.' About a week after
that, if I wasn't brought another late hatch, so
now I had thirteen again! Robert parted them; he
knew more about chickens than I did. Once chickens (hens) fight, they fight, and not only fight,
they'll kill each other's chickens. We never bargained
for the chickens really. Anyway, we put in a bit of
wire-netting fence and there were two hens in boxes
there."

"One night one of the little chickens from one
hatch had gone into the other pen, and when we
went down in the morning we found that she had
been battered. She'd been pecked. They only peck
the head, you see. There she was dying. I remember
crying over this poor little chicken, and wanting to
throw the other hen out. But she was useful to her
thirteen so we put a bit of finer wire netting between. Now, the chickens began to grow. And meanwhile so did the garden."

"We had leveled the top lawn . . ."

'Wal-Cum' was built on the side of a hill, with the
garden in front of the house falling steeply away, so
it was terraced on five levels . . .

" . . . and now he had got onto the second little
terrace. He leveled it well, that top. In order to
level that, he unearthed rock from one part of the
level to put it on the outer edge."

"Anyway, our garden was dug, and the chickens were growing. We couldn't let those chickens
wander, could we, around the garden because the
garden was growing? In the June after we arrived
we were reaping from the garden. That meant good
hard work. He'd done most of the back garden. We

169

had chickens from the word go, but now the chickens had to go out. Either the chickens had to go or he wanted to stop the garden. Well, it had to be the chickens . . . Meanwhile I talked to Owen of Llwyn'rhudol and Owen said 'You can put them in the Park land.' They were not allowed to use this parkland, only as parkland then. The war hadn't come to give the farmers liberties yet. So there was a little portion there (an acute angle corner between two walls) that was all refuse and had to be dug out. It was an old well with an entrance. Everybody from the gardens nearby had been putting their rubbish there. We dug up all that out and through digging; we took out a bit of root that was stuck in the wall. I remember pulling that root out and it made a little doorway through the wall at the bottom. We couldn't buy wood for love nor money then, because all the wood was going away to the war effort. So we kept all the box wood we could, and we went and bought five corrugated sheets of iron. We made the iron sheets the roof, joining over the two walls into the old well, and the doorway was, literally, made from old boxes. We could get into it when we stopped. The chickens had an entrance where the root had been and all we had to do to shut the door at night was put the stone back again. However, as it was near water, the rats were the trouble there really."

"Robert knew more about crime in London than he ever knew about rats. Now he had to learn all about rats. Also he had to learn about ants . . . and the ants beat him. He could not control the ants for years, for ages. He used to say, 'These damned ants, my Gosh. They're worse than any criminals.' He used to say that many a time to me."

"Now the children grew . . . the two little children grew and I never realized it. There were six and a half years in between. Jean was twelve. She had won the scholarship before she'd come to Wales.

*She went to the High School in Putney, for a year.
She was a very prim and proper girl; Jean was,
when she came to twelve years of age. Well, living
in the country, you soon drop your moves, and you
soon become that you don't want a hat, or anything else. From being a very prim girl . . . the
hardness with uniform wasn't so pronounced in a
way. They had to have uniform. She made three
uniforms in one year, Jean did. But she didn't have
to keep so strictly smart as she did in London. Now
I missed that with Jean really. Yet she kept that
reservedness all her time. She couldn't mix, though
she was twelve. She couldn't mix with the Welsh
people, like John did, which was a great loss to her.
Also the evacuees were coming now to Pwllheli from
Liverpool area, and from London. She would NOT
mix with them . . . the Liverpool people. They were
the poorer class then. From London, they were also
from Dagenham there you know (grimly); it was
not a good area then. But anyway . . . John mixed
with them better. Jean didn't. She was friends with
just one London girl though."*

The coincidence of Robert's 26-year retirement
with the onset of war, emphasized the change in both
their lives. Moving from the busy bustling city of London, in which they had been elements of a large
authoritarian force, the Metropolitan Police, to the
quiet of rural Wales and their own resources was a
very significant change in itself. The war underscored
their dependence on their own resources, and they
were able to make the adjustments.

Food rationing was put in place straight away. In
1939 different types of food – bread, meat, butter,
sugar, sweets, etc. were restricted to a weekly cou-
pon allowance. This rationing stayed in place for 14
years, until 1953. Edna had kept a few hens in

Wandsworth, London, and now they started with hens again. Later they added ducks, turkeys and pigs. Since Robert was immediately free to devote all his time to the land, he created a large productive garden with hundreds of fruit trees, apples, plums and pears, and fruit bushes, as well as a myriad vegetables. Once they grew an excellent crop of maize—corn to the US—but they had no idea whether it was edible, or, if so, how to prepare it. So, the hens were the fortunate recipients of the entire crop!

Edna had her flowers along lawns and paths but the garden was very much a 'Dig for Victory' effort. It later won an award as the finest in the whole of Caernarvonshire. Thus, with the exception of butter, sugar, milk and flour, which could be bought at local farms, they were self-supporting.

This was just as well because Robert's fixed police pension rapidly devalued during wartime inflation.

Another effect of the war was the organization of the populace. In the streets the khaki, blue and navy of the three fighting services, the brown of the Home Guard for last ditch protection of the island, and the green-jumpered Land Girls, who replaced farm workers who had gone to war, were all in evidence. Later there were Italian Prisoners of War and the Polish airforce. These groups all needed support: camps to live in, transport, and canteens for their hospitality. The country, even in this remote area of Wales, took on the aspect of War well before the air-raids.

> *"Everybody did their bit of war work . . . Robert*
> *also felt that he ought to do war work. He went as*
> *an Enforcement Inspector, but because he couldn't*

*speak Welsh, he couldn't get a job in Wales. He
was an Enforcement Inspector in Lancashire. The
inspectors stopped the hoarding, or black-market-
ing (in food) . . . only in food, not in anything
else at all. I think it was 1942. He was there two
years, but he found that he was he was very much
poorer with the pay he was getting than if he wasn't
working. So he came back."*

*"By this time we had got the chickens into the
park-land. While he was away, I was managing
the two children, keeping the house going, and also
by this time letting two rooms of mine to the navy,
in a way. This was for the benefit of the parents of
the very sick patients . . . on the danger list . . . at
Brynberyl Naval Hospital, just a mile away. It
was . . . the hospital for HMS Glendower naval
camp on the coast."*

Wives and Mothers not directly involved in the
war effort found plenty of opportunity for volunteer
work. Edna worked in the canteens for the service
personnel passing through. The Navy, Army and Air
Force Institute (NAAFI) and the Women's Voluntary Service (WVS) ran them.

*"Meanwhile. I was also helping in the . . . it
wasn't the WVS then, it was the NAAFI it
was . . . helping in the canteen where we fed the
men. I did it in two parts. We had the Liverpool
House canteen for the navy and the air force from
Penrhos. Then I worked in the Masonic Hall for
the women's part of the navy, the WRENS, and
the air force. Only the women came there. In that
place we had to cook and to make cakes and everything."*

*"We had very little direct contact with the war.
Very little, really. As far as we were concerned,
really, we had gone to Wales to escape from the*

173

*war. The war meant to us 'News of London', which
we knew so well. We had soldiers in the Yokehouse
camp; we had H.M.S. Glendower, the naval camp,
and the air force in the Penrhos aerodrome. We
also had the hospital, in which I now began to
take interest, in a way, because I was a member of
the Women's Institute. Women organized themselves, in many ways, like the WVS."*

Edna's work with the WVS was something she
chose to do on her own. It took her outside her home
and away from the family. She met other people every day and enlarged her own horizons and her views.
It was an independent activity — her first since her
marriage more than 15 years before.

While Robert was away in Lancashire, being in
charge with these outside interests, changed things
forever. Afterwards she really did contribute to the
decisions for the family. Still Robert would continue
to organize the garden, while Edna organized the
house and children, but in larger decisions of education, savings, purchases, and travel, equality was to
come after this war. For the moment, Edna didn't
see much change.

*"To me, the war meant very little actually. It
was only the upbringing of my children."*

*"We worked very hard on the garden. We had
bought that house with the garden on purpose to
have produce. Really and truly we were very comfortably off. We had plenty of food; we had vegetables from the garden. We never suffered from
real shortages. Also the Welsh people don't actually live like the English people. They don't even eat
like the English people. They didn't then. Their main
meals were cups of teas, cups of teas, cups of
teas . . . very simple. In Wales the quality of eating*

wasn't a very high standard (but) a very poor standard actually. So we had plenty of stuff in the shops because people weren't eating it . . . like cheese, and many a ration of sugar, and jam. I was supplied with sugar and jam, extra. Furthermore, we never suffered from lack of food because I could go to any farm and buy butter, and cheese. I had plenty of cheese and plenty of meat, and our own eggs, chickens and vegetables."

Edna's brother Willie had become a brilliant scientist who contributed to British research in the Antarctic. He worked in the Hudson Bay settlements and was part of the British Arctic Expedition inside the Arctic Circle in 1932. From that expedition he wrote a thesis and on the basis of the thesis he gained a Doctorate of Science. He was transferred in meteorological work to Cairo in 1935. He was 32. Let his sister, Maria, take up the story . . .

"Yes, he came back from Cairo, mentally ill, in 1938? Yes. You know the doctors on board ship; they wouldn't have it that there was anything wrong with him, you know. He was dual personality. They thought it was all wrong that they should be sent to accompany him all the way to Denbigh (the mental asylum.) He recovered sufficiently well to take up a job. What do you think it was? A doorkeeper! Yes, sad. Then he went from there . . . he was in Darlington then, you see . . . he went to King's College in London, to do maths, you know."

"Of course, in between, you know he was home in Maesnewydd. I was the only one who could . . . who was allowed to do anything for him. . . . He had a hankering. He wanted to see his old friends in Aberystwyth and he went there on his own, you see. He went to Aberystwyth on his own. He said 'Don't tell Gretta where I'm going.'

175

'All right,' I said, 'I won't. But she's bound to know. She'll want to know where you are.' So anyway, he went to Aberystwyth and when he got there, of course, his friend, a man called Davies notified the police. And of course, the police put him on the train back to Chwilog. They rang up you see. She told them in Chwilog that he wasn't very well, you see. So he came back. He never recovered fully."

"Willie was suffering from 'Change of Temperature Chemistry'; the chemical cells in the brain, you know. (It) changed their nature. Oh he was a lovely . . . well, I adored him, you know."

Eventually, his condition worsened and he became violent and was returned to the Denbigh asylum. Edna said:

"Now I was very troubled with the family, because Willie had a breakdown (in London). Robert had to go to London for Uncle Bill."

Maria continues:

"They (Emrys and Robert) had to go and fetch him from . . . what's the name of the hospital? No, he wasn't (difficult to restrain). Quite harmless."

Unfortunately that was not true. Willie was very violent on the 250-mile car journey back to Wales. It took one of them to drive and one to restrain. Later in Denbigh, as was the inhuman treatment of the day, Willie had a lobotomy, which turned him into a vegetable rather than the brilliant human being that he had been. This was not a pleasant time for any of the Morgans.

"All this time, two children were being reared.

Because we were busy we didn't realize that they were growing up into maturity, under our feet, under our noses. Now schooling too was much cheaper in Wales than it was in London. In 1944 Jean won her place in college, in the University (of Wales at Bangor); she went in for biology. Then in 1951 John also went to college to study mathematics. They both did very well."

Still everything at home wasn't always idyllic. There was occasionally the inevitable strife between man and wife. In this case it was the inevitable consequence of Edna having an independent say: even if it were only a slight independence.

"Well, put it this way . . . When Robert started on the garden, his son. John, was beginning to grow."

"There was the cinema. During the war they not only provided a cinema for local people, they provided it for the navy, and the soldiers of the district. Well, this cinema came in (opened), and Gretta (my sister Margaretta who was living in Chwilog four miles away) had an influence on Robert. She was saying at the time that it was wrong to teach John and Jean, to like a cinema . . . and not to love the country. But there were no two children that loved the country more, and who had been taken about by Aunty Mary (my other sister). Not only had we brought them to the country, but I personally felt that there was no harm in letting you go to the 'pictures'."

"Robert was listening to Gretta, really. But also, there was an unhappy time in SO Much as he thought that we were spending too much (on the ciema). At the time it was one shilling and ninepence for a second class seat. Things were getting tight. Our pension money was very much of a

muchness. *It never went up. It never went up until Robert was past 65. That was only nine years before he died. So money was scarce, and I was taking a few visitors in to help me to make ends meet. T'was no good saying that though . . . He was listening to Gretta."*

"In order to take the children to the pictures, I, many a time, collected sixpences in order to get three one-and-ninepences. For me to get three one-and-ninepences when the children were over twelve years of age meant an awful lot. I used to take them there and perhaps bring a few home-made cakes with me and a few home apples."

"All this time. Robert was digging in the garden not because we had to, because by this time the garden had been dug, but it had become a fetish of his, like earning in London. After he retired, it became a fetish of his, until one day . . . I remember quite distinctly this . . . I bought the children one of these cinematography books for Christmas. It was a cinema annual. He found that Jean and John and I could talk about this. He felt a bit out of it, and he clung to that book. He read and read and read the book, and in fact it was by the side of him always. He used to pick it up and read it."

This was Robert's way of joining in. He was too proud to want to go to the cinema with them, but he didn't like being left out.

"When I started taking people in, I didn't start to keep visitors for a business. All I did was (this). A matron came to the house at the time and asked me, could I put two rooms at the disposal of the relatives of sick people in the hospital. I never, during the war, charged them anything, until about 18 months after they'd been there. They would give me some little thing, say a pound. There were many

people from London, many people that came there who were too poor to pay. But I found out later . . . Matron told me at the hospital that I was entitled to three pounds per head for any person who came in the house. This money was given to the padre to distribute, and the padre had stolen the money! (He was staying with Miss Owen 'Bryn-Ynys'.) He ran away. Matron came in. She said 'Aren't you getting the money?' I said 'No, why? I don't get any money.' 'Well how are you managing?' I could have had supplies from the hospital. They said to me, if you are ever short of sugar or tea or anything. I was buying all these things. 'If you're short you can come and ask us', but I don't think I ever asked them for one thing. Somehow or other . . .

"Many times these relatives came without any clothes (to change). They were picked up off the streets of London. They were entrained to H.M.S. Glendower, and driven up to the hospital and then to us."

"There was a man and wife from Poplar who'd come . . . they were so poor. They had a son dying in the hospital. They came in on the Saturday. On the Sunday, they went out all day. Sunday I made dinner. Sunday night they didn't come in until eleven o'clock at night. They had gone as far as Bangor (30 miles away) to find a public house! They hadn't even visited their son in hospital! When they came in they were in an awful temper with each other. They hadn't eaten either. I remember bringing the dinner out of the kitchen oven, where I had tried to keep it warm. But I remember when they went back how grateful they were now. It was pouring with rain, the morning they were going. I got up early in the morning, went half way down to the town in order to show them the way to the station, these two people."

"All this . . . that I was keeping

visitors . . . was discord to Robert. I really wasn't keeping visitors (like in Towyn); it was a question of doing war work. Again voluntarily doing something."

"During that time, we had chickens. Now, our ration for chicken meal was very poor. In order to make ends meet then, I got friendly with people in town, and they said 'Well, it's all-right, Mrs. Graham, there is plenty of scraps in our house. Will you send for them?' John bach went round for the scraps twice every week. We were earning quite a lot from the hens, and selling quite a lot of produce from the garden. Robert put down all expenses that went to plant the garden, and out of the income, he was paid back. My chickens' (income) just went into the household."

Chapter 10

A Child's Wartime

Distances were longer in those days. At six years of age the small group of houses around 'Wal-Cum', a mile of fields away from the outskirts of Pwllheli, was a village in itself. It even had a shop; a counter in a front room where an old widow, Mrs. Hughes, sold groceries. The few houses poised on the breast of a hill were known as Llwyn'rhudol or 'The Enchanter's Grove', and although most of the houses were new in 1938, the name was not. It marked the junction of two ancient paths by which pilgrims traveled down the peninsular to a distant monastery on the island of Bardsey. In these days of the war, the paths were side roads, long by-passed by a modern coastal arterial highway, and a small feeder that passed by the front gate of 'Wal-Cum'. To a small child both roads led to distant places.

Pwllheli too was large then. It had been founded in 1152 by the Black Prince, mentioned in the Domesday Book and it now had 3,000 inhabitants. It was a surprise to John later to find that it was really a small town as towns go. On the Lleyn peninsular it had real importance . . . it was the market town at the railway terminus, and it was at least three times as large as any town within twenty miles. And that marked the edges of the world.

Robert, his Father, had bought the house from London and signed the final papers with a fine flourishing signature: 'R W Graham'. He always joined the R and the W. Mistakenly, the news spread around the neighbourhood that the house had been bought by a 'Rev. Graham.' Thus, since Llwyn'rhudol had no one of comparable stature, when Robert arrived with his wife and children he found that he was automatically the leader of the community! Coming from the capital of Britain: London, helped the mystique. It was some time before he and Edna found out why they were treated with such deference by the tiny community of retired sea captains and widows. Even when they found that he was really a Metropolitan Crime Chief the attitude didn't change . . . apparently policemen and vicars were of equivalent importance.

While his Father and Mother were laboring in the new garden; digging the soil and growing vegetables, and digging out the air raid shelter, John and Jean were growing. John remembers being introduced to work from the start. His job was to pick out as many stones from the dug soil as he could find. These went into a barrow and thence to the pathways. So pebble by pebble, stone by stone, and, later, rock by rock, the soil became fine and clean while the pathways were well drained and sound. John never knew that the game was either real or constructive, but in seeing his Mother and Father work together he got a good sense of partnership.

For his Mother, his Father had retired to Wales, her homeland, rather than to the North of England. For his Father, his Mother put her effort into the soil alongside him. The garden served them well; there were always vegetables to be had. On some days, John and his friends would fill small tin boxes with a variety of things to eat. They would collect one of each fruit: a gooseberry, a raspberry, a piece of rhubarb, an onion, a carrot, or a radish. Then they would retreat to the rocky hillsides behind the house to play Cowboys and Indians, knowing that they had enough food to last out for months if a posse followed them.

The countryside around was abundant too. In the summer, John would collect mushrooms with his sister. They went early when the morning dew still clung to the rushes in the low lying fields, early before the cows got up to wander across the fields stepping on the new buttons that had appeared overnight. John carried the tin urn to collect them, and they would come back with a quart or more to fry with bacon for breakfast. There is NO taste as fine as new mushrooms fried with bacon in the morning.

Collecting blackberries was more effort, but more profitable too. Again the tin urn would be filled to the brim with big ripe berries, several times in a day. The final collection would be bagged and taken into town for sale at the local greengrocers. John could earn three pence or sometimes even more from his share of the work. No one collected alone, the whole

183

family went down the favorite hedges, Robert would hold up the longest and prickliest branches with the curved handle of his stick, while the children would wriggle under for those largest and ripest of fruit. The end of a day's blackberry picking left everyone with tired backs, scratched hands and legs, and purple fingers and mouth. But it was worth it; the coins felt more valuable for having been earned.

Then there were days out. The family went to the mountains . . . three symmetrical hills about 1,500 feet high, called Yr Eifl. The English visitors later converted this to the 'Rivals' and wanted to believe that the threesome had some romantic history, however Yr Eifl resembled nothing more than the three tines of an old wooden pitchfork. On the summit of one there was real history, an ancient walled Saxon community, only ever visited by families like Robert, Edna, Jean and John on trips to gather 'llus'. The three hills were covered in bilberry (blueberry) bushes, and again the tin urn was brought into use to carry the luscious purple berries. John remembered the days as adventures. They cycled to the base of the mountains, climbed stone stiles to tramp up the mountain, far above the surrounding plain. At midday they sat deep among the llus bushes to eat cucumber sandwiches with orangeade. When he lay down the bushes would almost close above his head, and he would stretch out a hand for another berry that had escaped. He never ever quite remembered getting home . . . he was always asleep before reaching his bed.

There were plenty of other things to collect around 'Wal-Cum'. Down the hill, past the vicarage, long since empty, there was a small clear brook running across the middle of a field. If the bull hadn't been left in that field then you could cross to collect dark green watercress from the shallow waters. If the bull was there, then often times John remembers his sister Jean saying that they'd go for wild black plums on the hedge near the bridge instead.

Later in the year they would collect hazelnuts in tight clusters from bushes that had been marked by yellow catkins earlier in the year. There was one best place for nuts . . . on the old upper road to Pwllheli by the little church. Edna and Robert always walked in the afternoon after Sunday dinner, to 'walk it off'. Jean and John went along, sometimes willingly but most times very reluctantly. There were other things to be done, so going for a walk dressed up in 'Sunday best' clothes was no fun . . . unless the hazelnuts were ripe. John knew that when he got hold of a bunch, there would be three or four large hazelnuts held tightly in green pockets all joined together at one end. If you bit them, the taste was sharp and tart. The nuts were collected into Robert's deep pockets for later drying and eating close to Christmas. Edna would link her arms with Robert and know that they looked a smart pair, out for a Sunday stroll.

John helped in the garden while Jean worked in the house. They grew potatoes. In the summer they carefully planted individual seed potatoes, which had been left to sprout and hoed the rows into small mountain ridges, one after the other across the plot. It was John's job to follow his Father down the row with the box of seed tubers, carefully planting each so the sprouts were upwards. Later at harvest time, while his Father dug up the tall plants that had sprouted and grown through the tops of the ridges, John would follow behind stooping to pick the new white potatoes, to throw them through his legs into

185

a sack that he dragged along behind. He sorted them on the soil, first passing along picking out the large ones and then following with a second sack for the smaller spuds. John ended up grubby and dirty at the end of the day, but there was some satisfaction when Mum called in 'her working men' for lunch at mid-day, and he would eat a big plate of bubble-and-squeak next to his Father. He also got paid by the bag for this job, so he never missed a potato!

In the cabbage season, John also earned a little by catching Cabbage-White butterflies. He would chase across the garden with a large net of muslin at the end of a bamboo cane, and lay out the white bedraggled corpses, some with a touch of yellow in the wings, on the garden wall for counting. Each was worth a penny. That went on all summer and yet still small colonies of eggs were laid and still small green caterpillars hatched to make lacework of the cabbage leaves. There were more Cabbage-White's than could be caught with one net. Then John learned a first lesson. John found that after the corpses had been counted, Robert gathered them and threw them on the midden. If he took a few he could add them to the next day's catch, thereby making them each worth twopence or even threepence. It seemed a good scheme. Unfortunately, Robert was a policeman. He noticed eventually that some of the corpses were definitely beginning to fray, he might have even recognised a few at the count, but . . . payment stopped. John had killed the Golden Goose!

There was always a smell of cooking in 'Wal-Cum'. It came from the 'kitchen' where the family lived (not the back-kitchen where the cooking of meals took place.) There on the fire, three times a week would be an old five-gallon oil drum, which Robert had burned clean and equipped with an old pail handle. It bubbled away in a glorious sweet smelling mixture: food for the poultry. After it had cooked it would be chopped up with a 'masher' — an original tool invented from baling wire by Robert, and then mixed with a little meal. The hens loved it. The hot slightly-mealy smell was appetising as long as you didn't know what was in it!

During the war, the hens' eggs were sold to 'The Center'. This was the government distribution center. In return for the sale the producer was allowed to buy some meal for the hens, but it was never enough. Robert supplemented the food for the chickens from the hedgerows, gathering stinging nettles in large bunches. Edna arranged for John to collect scraps from neighbours. John hated it! Every Wednesday evening and Saturday morning he would go his appointed round, carrying two buckets for the scraps: bits and slops that he would find in pails put outside the backdoors. On the Saturday morning he cycled on his three-wheeler to the Naval Hospital a mile away, with a bucket on each handle. Many a time those swinging buckets would catch a knee and over he'd go. But it wasn't the work, or the slops, that he disliked most . . . it was the loss of Saturday morning. None of his friends worked on Saturday except for the boys at the farm. Very much later he recognized his small part in the supply chain. Starting from his collection, it was possible to keep the hens fed and laying. That meant that there was always an egg to eat for the family and the neighbours throughout the war when meat was difficult to get. The government strictly controlled the raising of stock and their sale in the cities because the usual British supplies of beef from the Argentine were cut-off by the U-boats.

They would hatch chicks and ducklings in the air-raid shelter and keep the small fowl in wire-netting pens on the lawns until they could be released in their small field. John loved the ducks. They waddled and quacked in groups. If you cornered one duck, you cornered them all. The hens on the other hand were unruly; a group of ten would scatter in ten directions. One year they had two turkeys. 'Sion a Sian' (John and Jean). They were large docile friendly creatures with a magnificence to which even a golden cockerel could never aspire. On the first Christmas, Sion became the chief celebrant. He tasted wonderfully after John had got used to the idea of eating a friend. Sian survived another year, and since she began laying, became a real friend of the family. The next Christmas, she was spared again while a stranger purchased from town was eaten. On the third Christmas however Robert hardened his heart and sacrificed Sian, who by now was past laying age. She was also old and tough! John felt that no one, whom they had come to know so well, would have tasted quite right.

The pigs also became friends. They loved to have their back scratched and John would hitch himself up on the edge of the sty to lean over for them. It was like stroking a tree and the harder he poked and scratched, the more ecstatic would be their grunts and squeals, and they humped their backs towards him for more. First one of the litter would eat more than the others and get fat enough to be sent to slaughter, and then the next would eat enough and grow largest in turn. The pigs never stayed around long enough to be on first name terms.

John never remembered having too little to eat. There were always enough vegetables and always an egg either fresh or preserved over the winter in 'isinglass.' Sugar, butter, meat, of course, chocolate, were the only items that he remembered being in very short supply. Many years later he was to read a report of a study that found that the healthiest Generation of British had been his own. This was because food had been rationed, and the quantity of each type of food was rationed in a balanced way. He was too young to know that how they ate was not usual, too young to know pre-War habits. Too young to realize the benefits of having some items curtailed!

John attended a Welsh school, six years behind his sister, Jean. While she remained 'English,' he was young enough to mix. The English schoolchildren evacuated from the cities, the 'evacuees' were educated in separate classes isolated from the Welsh (and John.) Integration had not been invented! Since John was not an 'evacuee' living in a foster home, but really lived in Pwllheli, but since he was 'English', but not as 'English' as the others, there was always some confusion as to whether he should be treated as a stranger or not. His school reports show that he did not excel in Welsh. He was solidly 23rd in a class of 26. Even his dancing outscored his Welsh language skills, although he privately ascribed his poor scores to Miss Roberts, a sharp faced harridan who would have fitted Dylan Thomas' most astringent descriptions. To be fair though, he didn't excel at anything in the lower classes, and he usually had a daily task of scratching penalty lines on his slate: 'I shall be attentive in class. I shall be attentive in class, I shall . . . ' He never managed to rank higher than 5th in any class until he was eleven.

During the war he could only remember being taught one thing of lasting value. He was whiling away extra time in his arithmetic class by drawing the master, Mr. Roberts of Chwilog (no relation fortunately to Miss Roberts.) Intent on his task he didn't notice that the master had seen him. "Bring whatever you're doing up here, John." He did. Then Mr. Roberts, after looking at his portrait, said slowly, "Never erase one line before you have drawn in the correct one." Mr. Roberts had taught one lesson indelibly.

During the war years the radio, a large polished wooden cabinet on a bookcase behind his Father's seat at the table, was their link with the world. They were momentous days, and the news took precedence over every other activity. Speaking would stop, mealtime noises would quieten, and John knew enough to stop playing. As Big Ben struck the hour for London and for the British Broadcasting Corporation, a voice would announce. "This is Stuart Hibberd speaking . . ." John's Father would brook no noise while we heard how the war was progressing. We knew too, instinctively, that all over Britain, and even all over Europe, there would be other families gathered around radios listening to the same news. It was the time when everyone came together. In his earliest years John was too young to remember how grim the news had been, even with the most hopeful of censorship. It was only later when General Montgomery had turned the tide against General Rommel in the North African deserts did it mean much to move the flag-pins, on the maps stuck on the kitchen walls, to show the progress of the armies. As the war moved to a close in Africa, moved up the leg in Italy and moved across the invasion beaches to the Rhine, the nightly broadcast ritual was a game of success. Only later when the whole family listened in awe to the Nuremberg Trials did John and his sister understand the monstrosities that had been committed. John heard Goering and Goebels declare themselves not guilty "Nein, Nein, Nein . . ." and at the cinemas saw the newsreels from Belsen and Auswitch.

Prisoners of war were housed in camps around Britain, and many did manual work in their neighbourhoods. The main camp near Pwllheli was at Fourcrosses, about 3 miles from 'Wal-Cum'. The camp, a temporary set of pre-fabricated buildings, which still remained 30 years later, had almost no security. The prisoners were Italians, mostly farmers who were more at home gardening for a few shillings than thinking of escaping to fight again. The gardener next door was an Italian prisoner. John remembers him as a kindly person who introduced him to coin collecting with a few lira coins. The prisoners were treated so well that after the war many refused repatriation and produced a small colony of Welsh-speaking Italians. They complemented the Welsh-speaking Poles who stayed after manning the Polish Air Force airfield on the other side of town.

Life during wartime for growing youngsters meant that some things were accepted as ordinary that in other days, other times might have been thought unusual. Early in the war a blackout was imposed; no lights could be shown at night for fear that enemy bombers could use them for navigation. 'Wal-Cum' had heavy black curtains on all windows outside the usual curtains. Each night they were closed and, checked from outside to avoid chinks of light. Car headlights were cowled with metal inserts allowing only a thin horizontal beam. The light was just good enough for the 20 miles an hour that the

191

cars could manage. John and his Mother many times walked up the long hill from town at night. Everything was so dark below that the stars seemed all the brighter. They watched the shooting stars scream across the Milky Way.

In 1940 everyone was issued with a gas mask. They consisted of a 3" filter cylinder attached to a rubber mask that fitted over the face, and which was held by adjustable straps. It had a clear plastic eye-shield to look through. John felt quite grown up to have his own gas mask exactly like his Father's. They were shown how to put them on by a Home Guard volunteer and they practiced to put them on quickly until all the exertion and sweating fogged up the eye-shield. Each night at home, and once a day in school, John would have to see how fast he could take the mask out of its rectangular cardboard box and put it on. As one breathed the rubber of the facemask would move in and out, and the air smelt a little stale.

A gas mask was a plus for a small child. John wore the cardboard box with its string over his shoulder all the time. It got in the way when he ran playing tag or chasing someone, but he got expert at holding it in one hand while the other was used to hold on to a classmate. One Christmas, John had a gift from his parents that eclipsed other gifts . . . it was a new gas-mask case: a blue pear-drop shaped container of plastic coated cloth into which the cylinder fit snuggly at the bottom to be followed by the face mask in the wide upper section. It had a wide shoulder strap. John thought it was fabulous and he was the envy of his schoolmates until they also got one to replace the worn out cardboard boxes. No one wondered at the oddity of giving a child a gas-mask case as his Christmas gift . . . Peace unto all men . . . and gas masks for the children!

Invasion was quite likely in the early years. Road signs disappeared to confuse the wandering foe, and Welsh descriptions were emphasised. The crossroad, 'Lon Groes', became 'Lon Groes Glyddyn' because it passed the 'Glyddyn' farm. When the signs were restored after the war they had changed to the new descriptions. There was a Home Guard too: a hurriedly assembled army of old men, women and sick, who could perhaps delay an invader with makeshift arms. They were trained with wooden weapons and farm forks, but they were very serious. Although they became the subject of much humour in the later years, it was exactly similar groups who were the backbone of resistance movements in less fortunate European countries.

There was also a camp of C-3 soldiers on the 'Yokehouse' farm. C-3 was the designation for the infirm and sick men who just, but only just, qualified for the regular army. They were lame, old, and many wore heavy thick glasses to accommodate very poor eyesight. They trained and marched in a side road close to 'Wal-Cum'. That summer was hotter than usual, and the thick serge uniforms left these men sweating and exhausted after marching up and down the lane. Edna sent John out with water for them. He carried it in the tin-urn that usually carried mushrooms and berries, and he sat on the ivy-covered wall until they had finished marching. Then the soldiers gathered around thankfully, and he would have to go for more. He did this many days in that summer of 1942.

In 1980, John was running a tape-recorded chess journal for the blind, and needing voluntary help to copy tapes he appealed among tape-recorder owners. One of the respondents was himself blind and doing similar work. That man, Charles Cadwell MBE, one hot summer, nearly forty years earlier, had been amongst the group of soldiers that were refreshed by the 9-year old.

Toys weren't available during these years, so Robert improvised. There was a billiard set. On the green baize cloth of the kitchen table, Robert provided a wood and rubber edging to form the billiard table. The balls were golf-balls and the cues were cut-down from real but broken cues. The rubber (taken from old bicycle tires) never produced the bounce really needed so John and his Father became expert at pocketing balls by semi-sliding them along the 'cush' into the pockets. It was a lesson in frustration but for one or two winters it provided hours of entertainment. The family played chess, draughts, and lots of card games. Close by there was a naval station and a hospital and there were always sailors or relatives staying at the house . . . 'the visitors' they were called. Edna always took pity on the young sailors, barely out of school, and while at 'Wal-Cum' they were over-fed, and, on their behalf, Edna cheated at cards. It was some time before she was found out; she would hand significant cards under the table to her guest. John never took cards seriously after that.

Edna was always kind to children, and she was never above cheating in small ways if the right thing resulted. It was never a rule, but an unwritten understanding that since food was short, and since the family made income from selling eggs, a single egg was a meal. It is almost, but often it wasn't quite. One evening, Robert was in town and two boiled eggs each appeared on the supper table for Edna and John and Jean. The thought of a second intact egg sitting there while he ate the first, dipping bread and butter into the rich yolk, was glorious. The second egg was an illicit luxury to cap off the meal. After, they were still sitting around the table when the door latch clicked. Robert had returned. Even though Edna by now was quite stout, she moved quickly enough to gather the eggshells, and use the poker to mix them into the coals of the fire. Robert came in after putting his coat in the closet under the stairs, and coming near the fire for warmth, he looked into the coals. "Oh, you've had two eggs tonight," he said. It was reprimand enough.

Robert's deductive logic came from his police-background. In retrospect some was quite simple, but at the time John felt there was nothing he could not discover, given a chance. Vegetables were grown from seed, and the sills of the south-facing windows always had boxes of germinating seeds in the sun in the early spring. They attracted young hands. One day, Robert accused John of disturbing the small plants, but of course, John was innocent. "It wasn't me," he said. So Robert took him to the offended seed box and placed John's small hand in the print in the soil. It fitted. It was unfair having a policeman for a father. It was only much later that John realized the significance of being the smallest in the household.

Clothes were hard to come by during the war. Hand-me-downs were the order of the day though in farming Wales that had always been true. New clothes could be bought with coupons, and Edna saved them until one of the children needed a new coat or a new pair of trousers. Some clothes arrived lease-lend from the USA. John hated them. He had

195

one atrocious jacket in navy blue with red piping around the collar and down the front. It had a long sloppy shape that labeled it as foreign and charity. It got dirty, and torn, quite quickly.

Edna also got flour sacks from the grocers. The smaller ones were almost fine linen. She cut them open to hem as handkerchiefs. Larger ones became variously curtains or sheets, but despite innumerable washings and dying in yellows and greens, the sacks never lost their original inscriptions. John was always blowing his nose on 'Enriched Flour . . . 5 lb.' which had originated in 'Pillsbury of Minneapolis'. Similar messages appeared as the sun shone through the kitchen curtains.

When the war ended rationing slowly ended and over the course of the next few years things appeared in the shops that the children had never seen before. Food rationing finally ended nine years after the war. Once Edna found lemons in Portmadoc and after queuing with others at the greengrocer's for some time she was allowed one (the limit). By this time both Jean and John were eagerly waiting to try it, and when Robert had cut it up they took their first traumatic suck of the fruit! It's a wonder they ever enjoyed lemon again.

The family attended the English Church in Wales: a sort of mild Methodist variant. Sometime during the evening's sermon there would be several loud cracks from the Graham pew. Then small pieces of strong white mint would be handed to the Edna and the children, and possibly even friends in neighbouring pews. Robert loved those mints, but they were difficult to get. They were about the size of a quarter, and he would break each into four pieces against-the palm of his hand. If Edna was ever

196

able to buy chocolate bars, then they too were cut into small pieces. The essence of luxury in later years was to eat a bar whole without cutting it first. When John was sixteen sweets came off rationing, and they could have more than the two-ounces per month allowed during the war. It was many years before chocolate was widely available but John's garden earnings had real impact when he could spend them on sweets.

When he had first come to Wales, Robert had intended to learn Welsh. He bought a small book entitled 'Welsh in a Week'. After a few months he retitled it to 'Welsh in a Lifetime' and afterwards his welsh was restricted to wishing the postman 'Bore da' (good morning), or thanking someone, 'Diolch'. Jean also missed the language, so John and Edna were always able to speak Welsh together when Robert or Jean were out of favor. In retrospect, this could have aggravated any quarrel, but at the time John and Edna shared a greater closeness than with the others.

Only the most unreal family will never have a quarrel of some kind. There was a period, after the war, when there was friction between Edna and Robert, and as usual John sided with his Mother (without ever knowing the argument) and Jean sided with her Father. Occasionally, it appeared as though violence would break out, though it never did. Still John felt impelled to protect his Mother, so once he hid his Father's police truncheon deep in the garden hedge even though it was never more than a souvenir. Much later he was large and strong enough to restrain his Father by holding his arms to his sides . . . the boy had grown up and his Father was getting older.

John's relatives were mainly his Mother's, staying

or living only four miles away in Chwilog. They were a hearty bunch, somewhat heavily built, substantial and well educated. Most had become teachers or something in healing: chemists or nurses. One, Uncle Willie, was a scientist. He heard a lot about Uncle Willie — Edna's favorite. Uncle Llew (short for Llewellyn) was short and stern, who surprised with kindness just when John had decided he should be obeyed, or else! Uncle Emrys was bald and good-natured. He had a crooked thumb with a thick cracked nail that had been caught in a mangle when he was a child. He was always ready for any sort of game and he always had a new puzzle or scientific problem. He might have been an entertaining mathematics teacher, but he never spoke to John about that. Edna's sisters all looked like her, all a little stout with roly-poly faces ringed by curly hair. Aunty Mary was the headmistress of a girls' school and she never forgot that she was an eldest sister. She could maintain discipline in any unruly bunch. She was not loveable but nice in a distant way. In a photograph that always stood in a tortoise-shell frame on Edna's dressing table, Aunty Mary is a kind smiling lady under a tree watching Robert on all fours giving John a ride while Jean looked on. Mary was caught forever with a family she never had.

Then there was Aunty Sophia, 'Sophie' she was called. She had married a Cockney grocer and had buried her operatic career in the dark boredom of the little house behind the shop. In these days she could have had her own career, but in those days she might have turned to drink. Instead she chose religion. She joined 'The Brethren' and attended revival meetings on the moors, and signed away her earthly goods to the elders of the church. When John knew her, she too was jolly and bright but a little given to religious advice at the oddest times.

Margaretta, Aunty Gretta, was the oldest. The house in Chwilog belonged to her. Her outlook was coloured darkly by the death of her husband at sea after only a few months of marriage during the first World War. She was a widow in fact and feeling; she had most of her family's love and warmth. Gretta and Robert were of an age however and they got on well; she was not above giving him advice for the benefit of her little sister, Edna!

Then there was John's favorite Aunt, Ria short for Maria, who lived a single and singular life, caring for everyone else in the family, one by one as they needed her. She never seemed to be in other than good spirits, always ready for an outing, a game, or a trip. She was closest in age to Edna. She had traveled throughout Europe from Leningrad to Italy and had even taken a trip on a tramp steamer around the Mediterranean. She was fun.

Even though they lived close by, John met the Aunts and Uncles fairly infrequently. On Boxing Day, and on birthdays, Edna and the family would go to Chwilog but these were formal times. John didn't like the trips much because there were no other children there unless Aunt Sophie had brought Trevor and Bronwen along..

Chapter 11

After the War

'*After the war, visitors (summer holiday makers) in the house started through people coming back for a holiday, after they had come during the war. Then there were recommendations: excellent connections actually. If I had left things alone it would have been all right but there was also discord behind in the kitchen. Robert thought there was no need to cook meals for the visitors . . . but there was, nobody knows better than I did. Robert not only wanted an increase in what we owned every year, but he also wanted to rear up children. He didn't realise actually what had to be done for any child until we had a grandchild in! He didn't really realise because he was away. Stop and think . . . he was on night duty all the time, and he was out. Men are out, they don't realise what is to be done.*"

In retrospect, Edna was simply becoming the leader in the household; the main money earner through her visitors, and she was able to spend some (albeit a very small amount) discretionary money on frivolities like the cinema, and books. She had less time to spend on Robert, caring for the visitors. Thus, much of the discord, especially during the summer season, came from an unhappy mixture of jealousy, and a feeling of being left out of things. In London, it had been different for Robert.

> *"In 1951, Robert broke his leg (in a cycling accident). He not only broke his leg, but he broke the confidence in himself, really. He was 61. He came to think of himself as not a perfect man. I'm sure that where a person breaks a leg and has no 'something to live for', they mentally deteriorate. It deprived him of a lot of interest, because he had been a keen golfer and a handy man around the place. Now, he took up, of all things, ironing! He used to say 'Pass me the odds and sods.' Bit by bit . . . it was a wonderful thing he did really . . . He was always handy in the house, in any case, but I can remember how he would sit up there with his broken leg and ease that leg up to save any swelling. Then he could take a frock of mine in his hand and iron it as good as any woman . . . better. He never put the iron down, that was the funny part. He couldn't relax and put the iron down and turn the frock. He was as handy with his left hand as he was with his right hand, and he would throw the frock over and smooth it in one movement!"*

Freud must have something to tell us about the situation! The jealousy for attention apparently gone.

The discord quieted, with Edna taking the leading part, while the older husband is reduced to 'doing a woman's work'! It was not quite as bald as that since they had always shared work in the garden or in the house, each doing what was most convenient. Now with a broken ankle that would not heal, Robert found one way to take his mind of it.

> "All this time the garden was growing and Robert's main interest was the garden, really? His life changed so much that he began to think that there was no object really, in doing quite so much in the garden. He used to say to me many a time . . . 'Well, we've got it well under control, I can carry on all-right, there's no hardship here.' He lost interest."

Then other calamities fell upon them . . .

> "Robert had terrible rheumatoid arthritis. He was terribly ill with that. It was only a year before. He was TERRIBLY depressed. TERRIBLY depressed with that. So depressed that I asked Doctor Charles and Doctor Gwenda if he had had a nervous breakdown. They assured me there was nothing of the kind, just a very bad illness . . ."
>
> "He only got better when I went to Holland with John. I had to go to Holland with John and his wife, Claire, only for a week and I stayed a week with them in Weymouth. During that time, I left Maria and Jean in charge. Maria, because Robert didn't want Jean to do anything personal for him. Jean was the daughter and Maria was the nurse. He was at a stage when you had to literally dress and undress him, and feed him. He was awfully depressed. He wanted me to go, so he made Doctor Gwenda sort of force me away (on holiday)."
>
> "Anyway, I went. The morning I went I broke

down properly there and threw the cortisone in the fire. 'These damned pills', I said. 'These are the cause of everything.' I threw them in the fire. 'You must never take them again.' So when I arrived at Chwilog . . . Maria had come and taken me to Chwilog to start on the train from there, from Afonwen. Before I went, I phoned Doctor Charles to tell him what I had done. 'I've thrown the cortisone away, because it was doing him no good. It's swelling him.' He was swollen terribly. He couldn't flex his hands . . . his face and everything. I had to practically throw him out of bed. I phoned to Doctor Charles. I told him he must come up at once and see him. That I had left home . . . or that Doctor Gwenda must come at once and see him . . . that I thrown away the cortisone tablets, that I felt they were wrong for him and that he must come up to see him. He assured me that it would be done. That was on the Friday morning, before nine o'clock, and they didn't go and see Robert till Saturday night. They were horrified to see the state that Robert was in, and they sent him to Bangor Hospital."

"I'd gone over now to Holland, and John wouldn't let me say a word about him. He didn't know how poorly his Father was. I was anxious about Robert. I didn't really want to come. In fact I was crying practically all the way to blooming London. But anyway, the thing was that I went to Holland and thoroughly enjoyed myself . . . Thanks to John and Claire at the time. So I forgot it in my enjoyment in a way. I didn't forget him either. I used to talk to Claire's mother, Mrs. Biggerstaff, about it at night."

"When we arrived home in London, there was a letter to say that Robert had been sent to Bangor Hospital 'for observation'. He had been to a specialist in Caernarvon. That specialist had previously told me this: that doctors were allowed, when

they had a certain number, say 40, patients of a certain age complaining of the same thing, to experiment! If they put them on a course of cortisone, or a course of another type of pill, those people on the pill might get better and stay better, or those people on the cortisone would have a recurrence. That's what made me suspect the cortisone. I forget the name of that other pill. But, anyway, eventually we arrived in Bangor to see him, only to find now that he had seen someone worse off than himself and it had done him the world of good, in a way! 'Under observation' meant that he was under the observation of this specialist."

"When he came back . . . it was most marvelous. Course Robert didn't want me to go and see him, but I went in with whatever doctor saw Robert. The specialist told Robert, 'It'll go away just as quickly as it had come.' I did get him out of the hospital before they were ready. I got him home. I thought 'I can make you better'. When he came home something happened . . . I had to go and get a stamp from his desk. I had been in the garden and I wanted to catch the post, so I had come in with a fork, a garden fork . . . I was trying to do something out in the garden. I came in and I said to Robert outside the back door, 'Hold this for a minute . . . hold this for a minute, I'll go in the house.' And I got a stamp out from his desk, put it on (the envelope) and now rushed off to the (postbox). Then I ran back into him and I asked 'Do you know where I put that fork? I knew I had a fork or something in my hand. Where did I put it?' I looked round, and I was absolutely horrified to find him with a garden fork in his hands; he was holding it . . . and he couldn't even use a knife and fork before, you see. I said 'Just look.'"

"What Doctor Gwenda was doing with patients like Robert was to watch the movement of the shoulder. It started in the shoulder. But they wouldn't

*explain what they were doing, they would tell them
to do something nonsensical. Both of us thought
that . . . Crikey! he's not so mental as to do that.
So the therapy didn't work. By the time he held that
fork . . . After that, I began to move him
now . . . not to allow him to sit in that room too
much. I began quietly to move him, with his arms
over my shoulder to the back door. Gradually, bit
by bit, when I moved him outside, he got better,
only by holding his own tools. That's what did it."*

*"Now he got better after that. He was surprised
how quickly he got better after he started getting
better. He still was despondent. There was that
despondency there that was never going to get . . ."*

Now, Edna, the younger by eleven years, was very
much the dominant character of the pair and leading spirit of the family. She managed on her own
without even mentioning the problem to John or
Jean. They had their own lives to lead. But the whole
of her own family began to look to her, as several
other things went wrong.

*"Then his brother died. His brother had been
very poorly in Sutton."*

*"Then Gretta broke her ankle. Maria, who then
lived with Gretta four miles away, was also in
plaster cast. She was the most cheerful spirit of the
lot, although SHE was in a plaster cast from shoulder to waist. Still, we began to get call, call, call
after call from Chwilog for help and I would have
to go there. Maria and I are next to each other in
age. Then just as for the first time in our lives that
Maria and I were feeling we could be more than
sisters, but be friendly . . ."*

*"Then that terrible thing happened . . . a lot
of illness and then to crown it all, if Gretta didn't
have a stroke. I was called again, and Robert had*

205

*to drive me. All this was no help at all. The care
that was to be needed for Gretta turned out to be
for the next seven years."*

*"During that seven years, things began to be
better financially, in a way. Robert was allowed
his added national pension. He hadn't been allowed to use it until 68 in 1958, because he elected
to pay more for a national pension for me too.
That again was a drawback. He had an increase
in police pension when he was 65, but since he
was paying for this national pension for me and
for himself, money had been a little short."*

Margaretta had, after her widowhood in about
1920, built a house in Chwilog, in the country five
miles from Pwllheli. Her house was named
'Maesnewydd', the new meadow, after the family
home in Towyn. After her parents' deaths, her home
became the home base for the other unmarried
brothers and sisters. Thus, Emrys and Maria lived
there intermittently, and William came when released
from hospital. At the time of Gretta's stroke, Emrys
and Maria were almost permanent members of the
household, so Gretta had no lack of help. Unfortunately Emrys was a sponger from way back. When
there was any work to be done, he was elsewhere.
When there was a copper to be made, he would ap-
pear. He was always full of 'get rich quick' schemes
that involved others' investments in money or labour.
Thus, Maria had to cope with Gretta who had a stroke,
William who was released occasionally from the asylum, and Emrys who made more, not less, work. When
Edna went to help Maria, she was treated much as if
she was the servant back in her Mother's home forty
years earlier.

"All this time we were going backwards and forwards to Chwilog. It became a real burden. I wanted to get out of it so I said one day to them 'Now you can manage here. You have Willie and Emrys and Maria. There's no reason at all why I should sit up at night. One of the men can sit up at night with you.' None of them did. Anyway, I went away. I came back home. I had been six months with Gretta. During that six months I only came back to clean and to wash for THEM in my own home . . . carried all the washing. Bit by bit, we could see that we were being imposed on. Our house became the washhouse for Chwilog. One day, Robert told them 'No more'. I told him. I'd stand by him if he said it. So he did. 'Edna's not going to do anymore. We're not going to do anymore.' We told Ria this. Next day we went to see them, only to find that they had rushed out and paid 100 pounds for a washing machine, which they could have bought before!"

"But now Maria was going under. I could see Maria going under, and I tried to tell her that the washing machine was now a penalty for her. She had to stand there washing and the more this washing machine washed, the more she had to iron. Gretta by this time was . . . not incontinent . . . she was . . . a lot of cotton wool was used. We used to visit them. Robert used to sit with them and I'd do ironing. I used to iron solidly for four hours and then I hadn't finished ironing."

Even with the automatic washing machine and the new non-iron fabrics, it takes people years to accept labor saving innovations. Many a woman would not trust non-iron fabrics. In Gretta's house, eventually the group bought a small refrigerator and said they were very pleased with it although the lamp inside didn't work. Then Robert discovered that the

207

refrigerator was being used as a cupboard in which to store milk and food, but it wasn't even connected to the electricity – it wasn't plugged in. Typically it is twenty years between an invention, and the full public acceptance of the invention.

However, better days were to come for Edna and Robert. They were being introduced to foreign travel.

> *"When we had broken free of the family at Maesnewydd, Robert and I would go out together. As money became easier he became more relaxed, and when I stayed with him longer he became kinder. He realised too that the children were building their homes. We had decided years ago that we were never going to be a trouble to our children. He said it many a time. He also said 'The children don't want us. We will never be needed by them, so we'll just cling together.' Sometimes when I used to feel a bit depressed about something or other he would say 'Well, it's all right, Ada, you've got me.' We used to go out, arm in arm, with two walking sticks, and I used to say 'Well, we've got two walking sticks and three legs, haven't we, Robert darling?' That's how we were, and we were very happy. The last two years he was the man I knew before. He'd recovered and he used to brag about it. He was so pleased."*
>
> *"After I'd been to Holland, we were together in the house and the winters are long. When you've got no Women's Institute, no nothing . . . we would talk, and I would tell him all about Holland, and show him the pictures. Then the second year John asked him if he would come. Oh no, he wasn't going to come at all. HE went to Jean's . . . but when he took me to the bus to go up to London, I could see tears in his eyes as he waved me off. By the time I was going after he had refused, he wanted to come. He did give me a little money that time to*

come. *After that holiday I talked and talked about Switzerland! There was nobody else to talk too, so he listened, and he was taking an interest. I asked 'Well, will you come one year, with me?' He always said he wouldn't go to Europe because he hadn't seen enough of England.'*

"The third year, John asked us to come, and this time he didn't wait. He just sat down there and then, wrote back and said he was coming. Now this time, when we got back . . . it wasn't me saying anything at all, I was quite quiet . . . when we went out to anybody, he said how he had beers abroad, and how his son did this, and son . . . And what's more, he said 'Next time, I'm not going through France, but I'm going to fly.' To my horror then he decided (laughing) to look up the brochures as early as January . . . after Christmas it was . . . "

"Now money was better for us, with no children and the pension . . . I was getting supplementary pension then, and Robert was getting the other . . . we decided now the children were settled, they were starting their home and we could start spending. Money became of no value to him. He would be like this . . . He would take out of his pocket a bundle of notes and say 'Do you want it?' I said 'No, I don't want it.' 'You have it,' he'd say, 'money is of no value.' He would give me 5 pounds just like that, and a ten-pound note he would give me. He liked giving. When he gave, he gave. He was generous when he gave. He gave me the house, you see.'

So they began their big adventure, a vacation abroad on their own, coupled with their first flight ever. They were together just savoring one of the fruits of this century's technology . . . at last they had the time and money to do so. For the moment too

Robert was back in the driver's seat, though Edna was content with that.

"When he flew . . . he got all the arrangements through a Caernarvon agency. They weren't answering him quick enough, and . . . Well, anyway, when we flew to Basle, he was in his glory, absolutely. You never saw anything like it. We didn't worry about anything. When we got as far as Basle we were allocated to our coaches. Robert and I had arranged quietly to be together, to sort of lean on each other. And we were sitting behind two people who were absolute snobs. They wouldn't talk at all. There were two behind us who did talk with us. We were going to be together, we were not going to part mind you, but we were going to be friendlier, cause John had told us how to be friendlier. And never to talk out loud, so by this time we weren't talking loud either. We were watching people."

"When we went to Italy, Robert felt he knew a bit of Italian and German. When he would try to . . . fair play, he would get these little books out. I never thought of getting the book out. I sort of made my signs somehow. I got on better without a book though. But he liked it; he liked being on his own now. On the second day, it was June 3rd, and we woke up hearing the running mountain water, and he was a different man from that time onwards . . ."

"He was absolutely on top of the world. We were going up on one of those high passes, and Robert was very sensitive. He whispered to me, he said 'There's something wrong with this coach. The brakes . . . the brakes are not holding.' I said, 'Forget about the brakes . . . 'Now we thought our driver on that coach was a German. He had a German head. He never spoke a word. But our courier on that coach was Peter; he was as lively and bright

as any. Anyway, Robert passed the courier and went to the driver. You never saw such a surprise in all your life (laughing). He was on top of one of these passes, and he was starting to talk to this driver to explain about the brakes, and this driver was as Cockney as they made them. He wasn't a German at all but a real Cockney. By Jove, before five minutes, he was telling Robert . . . whispering to Robert that 'Yes, the brakes were bad'. They were wrong on that bus, but it was all right. He would see that everything was all right. He said 'Jolly glad to hear that you were a Metropolitan Policeman', and all the rest of it. Well he said. 'It's all right we've got duplicate brakes on this bus.' By that time we didn't care what happened, we were in good familiar hands."

"I remember going towards Genoa, seeing all these rice fields, and these long long autostrada through there . . . and these rice fields . . . how low they were, really. How very wet and damp they were. And it was dry weather, although there had been snow on top of the mountains. Beautiful snow there. There was snow falling I mean. But anyway, when we arrived in Italy now, his only idea was to put his feet in the Mediterranean. That's all Robert ever wanted to do in Italy, really."

"We had a wonderful hotel there, lovely hotel, BUT in that hotel the noise in the morning was awful. If we had been another week we'd have enjoyed it better. A week is not long enough to be on one of those tours, really, in one place. We went away for two weeks, but one week we were being driven, if you notice, and one week we were actually there."

"I'll tell you what now then, we were warned before we went into it that we were not to be scared. No English driver is allowed to take his coach into Italy, so we were warned not to be afraid of the way that the Italian drivers drive. Well, you can just

211

imagine what Robert was like. When the Italians drove, they drove round those corners . . . just absolutely whizzed. By Jove, he was bad with the Italians, and the Italians didn't take a bit of notice of any of us. They are the best drivers, aren't they? Reckless drivers."

"Anyway! Now, when we went to Monaco, the country where Princess Grace lives. We recognized the place from John's photographs. Our courier was really for two buses and he didn't tell us everything, as he should have done. So I said 'Oooh! That's Princess Grace's Palace.' I said, 'I know it is, I know it is. It's . . . Don't you remember John's picture on the wall?' It so happened that a stranger was by my side, and he said 'John's picture on the wall? It doesn't look like that Palace, that's Prince Rainier's Palace.'"

"Anyway, later that day we were going down to where you gamble . . . Monte Carlo. We had to go to three different countries that time and Robert had forgotten to bring his money and passport. Anyway, we were allowed through and I had money. Now Robert was, by this time, in a holiday mood to try the casino. He was in shirtsleeves on holiday, but my gosh, he was sent away from the Casino, to put his coat on! They won't allow you in. Anyway, I did try. You buy these tokens and put it on a number. You know there was a woman by me, and she pushed me off. I was only one space from it, but she pushed off. You've got to say your result very quickly. If you don't say your result quickly another person can claim it. It's terrible. This woman pushed me off. I think I put it on 2 or 2A or something like that. Anyway it was a toss-up between her and me but I wasn't quick enough in shouting. She pushed me off. Well anyway we had a bit of fun over that."

"Going back through the countryside, the asters growing there were beautiful, really. But our journey was spoilt because we were going too far a distance and too fast. We were racing through . . . not like when we were going with John and Claire in their car. They would tell us, and stop, and tell us. We missed them very much that week. We felt that if we'd only had a car, we could have gone quietly, and we could have seen far more. Also we had learnt too that the beaches weren't free in Italy, not at all."

"Now, on our journey home now, the day we were returning, we were being taken to Basle. At St. Gotthard . . . We were asked whether we would like to go through the tunnel under the Alps, or to go over the pass. The bribe was that if we went through the tunnel we would have more chance to go to a very good hotel at the other end. Well everybody wanted to go over the passes. We went through the tunnel, though. But the reception at the other end was absolutely superb, and going through the tunnel IS an experience."

"When the plane took us over, we were two parties. The other coach went to the foot of Italy to a different part. We also met other people for our charter plane that had gone to the foot of Italy. They were glad to get into the tunnel out of the light. They had been very very ill. They had food poisoning. Also other people who had chosen more popular places, along the coast there, had part of their holidays spoilt because they had to pay so much even to go on the beach. It's terrible."

"In our case we didn't have to pay anything like that. We enjoyed it in so much that at the end of the week we were getting used to the po-licemen, and the people in the house. I think in a second week we would have thoroughly enjoyed *it, because we would have learnt then to go about a bit on our own."*

"Coming back home from Basle we had arranged to go on this holiday again. That was actually only two years before Robert died."

Chapter 12

Independence

'Wal-Cum', its land and livestock was suddenly too large for a retired couple, and would be even more so for a wife left behind. Robert started to close it down. Large areas of vegetable garden were put down to lawn in easily cut levels. Most of the land open to poultry was restricted and the land given back to nature. Changes around the house to steps and pathways were made to ease Edna's life alone. Robert was quite healthy, but anticipation, that his 11-year younger wife would have to live alone, was a real one.

"The next two years we were still worried by Gretta, all the time calling us at twelve o'clock at night. Two o'clock one morning, it wasn't fair. Also

*we were worried . . . they were phoning next door,
and upsetting things. (They had no phone in 'Wal-
Cum.') I could see Robert getting
paler . . . definitely getting paler. The year that he
died, 1964, we had decided to go away. We asked
Jean if she would come with us and she said 'No.'
He was disappointed at anybody saying 'No' then.
Anyway, (tiredly) we were sorry for Jean, that she
wasn't getting decent holidays or anything. The
thing was this . . . he did try, he wrote for . . . some
pamphlets for Switzerland. He would start in the
morning and we spent many an hour after breakfast after the post came in, just looking and talking together. He would start, and it would drop
out of his hands. We never decided on anything.
He even got so far as to decide where we were going
to no, but I could see the interest dropping, looking back I could see the interest declining, but then
I didn't because he was the leader, wasn't he? He
was the man who would decide, like John. We had
to rely on him, in a way. I was relying on him."*

Habits die hard. Edna had relied on Robert to
take the initiative and to make the decisions for the
last 40 years. Now she was the dominant personality
in terms of everyday decisions, but she continued to
THINK of him as the leader. She still needed his
'decision' for the unusual event like a foreign vacation. Today, the equality of man and woman in a
marriage partnership wouldn't allow this sort of dependence – the stronger would take the place of
the weaker.

*"He began to feel very much better. His health
improved tremendously. You would never believe
it. He would go out and he would do things and
he would say: 'No, you can't go to the back of the*

216

*garden today, because it's too windy. We'll go and
work in the front. Have you got a job in the front?'
We'd go together. Soon as we weeded one flower bed
together, we did our work together, and we were
really enjoying ourselves, simply working together
by this time."*

*"We'd go to Criccieth. I found he was sleeping
in the car a lot. While he was waiting for me, I
saw him once in front of the Post-Office fast asleep
at the wheel. I began to think . . . he was going
slower. One day when I was in Chwilog he came
and told Gretta that he'd been to Doctor Margaret
and that she'd told him that he'd got angina. From
that time onward I was more with him than ever.
If he was told anything he would dwell on it, and
he was dwelling on this angina, deliberately going
slower, which was right."*

By this time, Robert was 74. He had had an active life and by what we know now there was absolutely no need 'go slow'. It would have been better
to do the opposite if anything. But then the 'wis-
dom' of the age was to take care and hope for a few
more months. The damning thing about this 'wis-
dom' was that it destroyed hope, and it is hope and
expectation that keeps us going . . . at any age. Dylan
Thomas, the Welsh poet, put it into words for his
own Father. He said: *"Do not go gentle into that good
night, Rage, rage, against the dying of the light."*

*"Foolishly, Emrys got hold of him one day and
tested his eyesight, and he told him he had double
cataract in his eye, . . . in the pupils of his eyes.
From that time onward too he dwelt on that. That
was fatal to Robert. Well his sight WAS going. He
was 74, but unfortunately the Graham family, as
a family, dwell on sickness. There are some people*

217

*that you mustn't tell anything to, and (indignantly)
who was Emrys to tell in any case? When I heard
that he'd told him . . ."*

*"During this time Emrys tried to get him
glasses. I kept saying 'Don't listen to him. What
does he know about things? He's only trying to get
a cheap job,' I said. So he went to see Doctor Parry.
My gosh alive! there was a controversy! We didn't
know anything about it, mind you. It seemed that
Emrys had examined him before his two year's pro-
bation (as an Optician) was up. Emrys had done
wrong. It got Doctor Margaret into trouble. Because
Doctor Margaret had recommended that Robert see
Doctor Parry. There was an awful schmozzle about
it. Well. Anyway, I could now see too that the sight
was going."*

Edna had never driven. She now had the sense
to realise that it was becoming vital that she should.
She could not depend on Robert as much. 'Wal-Cum'
was a mile and a half out of Pwllheli uphill, and the
local Crosville buses were few and far between.

Robert had learnt very much by trial and error
and was never a good driver . . . he had acquired too
many bad habits. He could never be cured, for example, of careering madly downhill in neutral in
order to save a little petrol. It had been useful during the wartime. Neither could he TEACH. A standing start with a manual gear on a hill demands that
the driver know when the car is about to move forward. He knew, but didn't realise he was listening to
the engine change tone. Thus, he was intolerant of
new drivers who had been taught in different ways.
Edna was in for a rough time.

*"Now we decided to do away with our car. I
think it broke his heart too when the car went: the*

218

old Ford Prefect. *Although we knew it was ready to go. The new car, a Ford Anglia, wasn't to be delivered until we came back from Italy. I was trying to get him to say that I could drive. Learn to drive. I'd seen an advert in a cinema about one of these instructors so I said 'Shall I go?' 'All-right, all-right.' he said. He takes me down in his car, and I'm to learn on the instructor's car. I go for the whole of that winter on the instructor's car. When I decide, on my own, to take a test . . . I wasn't half ready . . . the instructor said 'Now we'll start in your car.' You can just imagine the schmozzle even to get Robert to let me have it! Eventually I got permission from him to take the car one Sunday morning."*

"When I watched him drive I found that Robert wasn't even driving our car right. I was saying 'It's not that way, it's this way.' The Highway Code came up . . . the driving code came up . . . he was beginning to read the driving code . . . The thing was this, that he didn't understand the car either. Anyway, I would have one or two lessons from him with him in the passenger's seat. He had never been in the passenger's seat. It was a question of always 'Keep in the middle of the road. Keep in the middle of the road.' So I never learned to drive. Whenever he was in the car I had to keep in the middle of the road, and the other instructor was telling me to keep on the left of the road."

"I don't think that helped his heart. In fact, I know it didn't, because . . . he never kept a diary as such but this year he did. The last year he lived, and in that diary, is all about how 'The ticker is not too good. I suppose it's going out with E.'"

"I never saw that diary until afterwards. I used to know sometimes. 'Why don't you rest? Why don't you rest properly? Why don't you go on your bed?' Sometimes he would go on his bed. But he would always say 'No, I can't let you go on the

bus. I must come and drive you.' I used to say 'There's a bus going at quarter past two, I can get the bus, and get my goods.' 'Oh no, I'll drive you.' He was like that; he was driving himself if he only knew."

"When we would go to the town, he wouldn't let me walk with him because he knew I was walking too slowly with him. But really although I was younger than Robert, I had got used to his pace. I didn't mind. Time was nothing: no value to us then. I didn't mind how slow I was. About a week or so before he died (very sadly) he got terribly cross-tempered with me in town there. Would I go on ahead, he would be coming. I used to miss him during that winter."

"But then, his sister, Mary, in Canada died. I had been out and when I came home I could see him coming from the garden with his head down. Instead of him saying to me 'Are you tired, Dear?' I said to him 'What is the matter, Robert?' I saw him terribly pale. 'What's the matter, Robert?' He said. 'Mary's dead.' You see. And I put my arm in his and we went inside and we cried and we wept about it. From that time onward he was terribly depressed until the day before he died."

"A few days later, we were invited to Jean's for a fortnight."

Edna's daughter Jean was living in Bangor, a University town about 30 miles away, with her husband, Gwyn, and her 8-year-old son, Clive. Gwyn was teaching mthematics in the Bangor Normal teaching college.

"For some reason or other he didn't want to go there. He tried his level best not to go there. He didn't want to go. Whether he was too ill . . . I think he was too tired. It so happened that that

morning Robert that we had a letter; little Clive had had mumps. We thought of using the mumps as an excuse for not going, but Clive wrote 'Come on, Taid' he said to his Grandfather, 'Come on Taid to stay with me because my mumps are better and I've got a good appetite. Come and stay and bring your penknife.' So we decided that we had to go."

"That morning I developed a cough. He was to take ME to the doctor, but I wouldn't go unless he had 'that little pain' examined. He had said that morning, sitting on my bed, 'I don't know, there's just a little pain there.' He just didn't want to go. Whether it was too much trouble I don't know . . . I think he was fed up with everything, I don't know."

"Robert wanted me to have a smaller house and whenever we did look for a smaller house we'd come back, and we'd always say 'What can you (get) better than this, in the end.' That's all we thought of. We thought, well the upstairs is empty and we didn't worry about it. We were living, and living quite happily together. We ought to have arranged the house as a downstairs flat. Then we could have done it. But we had then put the house on the market."

"The day before I never saw him in better spirits. On April 3rd he was wonderful all day. The day before an estate agent told us that he wouldn't let anybody come without him, but nine people called that day. That in itself was enough to upset Robert. Nine prospective buyers. We went out in the afternoon, and he was wonderful, honestly, all afternoon."

"But it was a bitter day, a bitter day. By this time he had even arranged in his mind that fires were no good . . . and he kept the electricity on. But where's electricity with two older people? Really and truly you must keep the rooms warm

too . . . *especially since Robert was a cold mortal. I
felt cold, and when we came in that night we only
had an electric fire going in one room with the oil
stove in the hall. It was too late for Robert really, he
had a meal afterwards, and his meal was a fish
lightly cooked in milk, with cheese sauce over it. He
liked that meal but actually it was too late. You
couldn't give Robert a late meal. Nine o'clock was
much too late. But he was happy (choking). I never
saw him happier. When he was happy, he would say
'Cut my hair.' And he was sitting having his hair
cut, and there we were laughing and joking, and I
said 'Now let me see, let me see.' I'd say. I'd count up
the haircutting charge they would make on mine,
and that night I remember saying 'Twelve and six,
that is, my boy.' And he would just smile, and laugh."*

"*He came upstairs and he felt cold. He was used
to putting an electric blanket in his bed at six. That
night he was coming to my bedroom because we'd
started spring cleaning his room. He went upstairs
to bed. Now he was nervous, ever since his illness, of
going to the bath, so that night I bathed him. I cut
his hair, and bathed him, washed his hair and he
was warm as toast going into bed. He had the electric
blanket put into my bed, and he lay where the electric
blanket was. And there were two bottles waiting for
me. When I went to bed, I said 'It's like old times
isn't it?' We were laughing and larking about you
know. We were really happy. In the middle of the
night I must have wakened up and I said 'Now what
in the world have I done wrong?' Meaning in the
car I was. He put his arm round me and he said
'You haven't done any wrong. You turn over.' he
said. 'You don't do wrong. You haven't done any
wrong.' I must have gone to sleep. I heard the clock
strike four . . . and he said 'I can't leave this house
you know. I'm getting too old.' 'I know you can't,
Robert. I'll write to that old man (the estate agent) in
the morning, and we'll cancel whatever he's doing.'*"

> *"When I woke up, he said to me 'Quarter to eight, Dear.' He used to say, 'The Towyn train . . . '"*

The Towyn train chugged below the house down towards the coast from Pwllheli on the right around the bay to the left. It was the first of the day, a sight to set time by.

> *"I said 'Yes, all right, I'll get up. Now you stay in bed and lie for a bit. I'll go.' 'No, no,' he said, 'You lie in my arms for the next quarter of an hour.' So I lay and like old sweethearts we were. Then I got up, and I said 'Well, I'm going to feed the chickens. NO, I won't feed the chickens.' I said, 'we're going to have breakfast first. I'll write that letter to that old man, the estate agent Kane.' I got up and went downstairs and started getting break-fast. The usual run was that he would go and feed the chickens, and I would go and make the break-fast. Well this time we reversed it and we wrote letters. I went later to feed the chickens . . . I posted my letter, and he'd written another. He said 'Put that on top of the clock and don't touch it for three days in case anything happens.' I didn't even know what letter he'd written, so I took hold of the letter from his hand and put it on top of the clock, where he used to keep anything like his change of glasses or his purse. I left that letter on top when I went to feed the chickens."*
>
> *"When I came in . . . now this was most unusual . . . normally if I went out he would clear the table . . . we worked together everywhere, what-ever I didn't do, he did. When I came in, I found a tray put crossways on the corner in that little back-kitchen place. I thought 'Well, he must have run upstairs to get ready to go to take me to the doctor.' And the horrible thought was that I was to drive the car backward out of the garage! And I*

had pleased him so much the night before, but I
was scared stiff of taking the car and reversing out
of the garage, and down a hill. Oh, I was simply
terrified. I was really and truly delaying things so
that he would drive me down."

"Well, I went alone the corridor, and found
that the middle room door was open and the sun
was shining through. Turning round, I saw that
the big leather chair had been moved into the window, and I could see was Robert's head over it. I
said 'What's the matter, Robert Darling?' And I
went up to him and he said 'I think I've had a
little something . . . a heart attack or something.
I've had terrible indigestion. I've taken some indigestion tablet but it hasn't worked. And Doctor
Margaret's tablet's not working either.' He had tablets in his pocket for about two years . . . three years,
I think, that he could take. But he'd never taken
them. And I said 'Well, never mind. You sit down
for a bit. You must give time for a thing to work.'
And I sat down on my knees by his side, bringing
now the fire nearer to him. But I often wonder if
I'd only taken . . . we used to have brandy for emergency, but he wouldn't have done a thing. Looking
back I think of these things. Now then, I said 'Well,
anyway,' I said quite pleasant really, 'We can't go
to the doctor!' What I was thinking was that I
needn't drive that car out backward, and I was
smiling really with him. I said 'We can't go to the
doctor. We'll have to get the doctor to you, won't
we? Now you sit down there.' And I put his feet up
on that puffet. And off I trip next door to phone
the doctor. She asked me whether he was in bed,
and I said 'No.' 'Well, will he go to bed? I'd like to
see him in bed.' When I came back to him, I said
'I've phoned Doctor Margaret.' And this time he let
me help him out of the chair. Robert was always
very independent; he would always help himself.
He let me help him out of the chair, and I put his

arm over my shoulder and we were going upstairs,
and I was laughing and I said "It isn't often I've
had to put you to bed on Saturday morning, is it?'
He could enjoy a joke, and he was smiling but I
knew it was a tired smile. He didn't look right,
somehow."
"Anyway I got him to bed and he asked for his
bedsocks. It was nothing new for him to ask for his
bedsocks. He liked his bedsocks. That day I had
taken the bedsocks downstairs to be washed, be-
cause he had decided by this time to go to Jean's,
after of that letter in the morning. I put his bedsocks
on. I got two bottles in his bed, and I made him sit
up in bed with a lot of pillows. He was sitting up
and I said 'Now you look nice and comfortable for
any doctor to come and see you.' 'Then he asked me
for his gold watch . . . a thing he never asked for. I
brought the watch and I said 'My Gosh, not only
do you look smart.' and he was smiling, 'but you
want to be dressed up too, don't you?' And I put
his gold watch on . . ."
"I was fastening it, when Doctor Margaret
came in. Seeing the door open she walked up. Then
she examined him and asked if he would go to
hospital and she turned round to me and she said
'Mrs. Graham.' she said, 'I want you, in half an
hour, to phone to the hospital.' (Brynberyl this was.)
'To see if there's a bed there, and if not, will you
send down for this prescription.' As she mentioned
the prescription, she said the word 'D . . . '. This
word 'D . . . ' properly upset Robert. As soon as
she went away he said 'What's she putting me on
D . . . for?' He knew Gretta had had it all the time,
this D. . . . 'Well,' I said, 'it must be something for
the heart, not as important as Gretta. You've got
nothing the matter with you like that, have you?'
But he began to worry . . . by saying that he was
too heavy for me, and that the ambulance men had

225

to do this, and if they were taking the weight . . . and
all the rest of it. He was worrying about the D. . . ."

"I went a little later . . . half an hour . . . to
find out if there was a bed, only to be told that
there wasn't. I came tripping back, and' I said.
'You'll have to have the old matron, Robert. I'll
have to get that book out now from the bookshelf,
and' I said get on my apron.' I said. 'We've got a
better home than any Brynberyl.' He smiled and he
was ever so pleased, quiet. He'd had a dose of
P . . . from Doctor Margaret, and you could see by
this time that he was resting and tired. Quiet now."

"I had given the prescription to the man next
door to go down town for it, when I phoned. I left
Robert to sleep there and he looked very happy. I'd
already packed his things to go to the hospital. He
would take his everyday lather cup to hospital, not
his nice things for shaving. He said he didn't mind
going to Brynberyl with a cup at all. He said he
was going to have his cup, his proper cup for shaving."

"I happened to go back into the room for something, and I saw his colour changing. I wish now
I had stayed with him, but he was, as I thought,
going to rest. When I went up a little
later . . . twenty minutes later . . . I found that his
arm had come out of bed. He'd taken his false teeth
out and the arm was down. I thought he was asleep,
through the dose. I took his arm and I put it in
bed. I put my arm around now to see the bottles
weren't touching him, and that he was warm, and
I whispered to him (choking) 'Well, you must keep
yourself warm you know Robert.' I whispered to
him. I kissed him. Then I knew he'd gone
(crying) . . . and I ran down . . ."

"Everybody came. They asked me to go out,
and I said 'No, you don't. No, I won't go out.'
Then Doctor Margaret came up and I went down
then, you see. (Crying) It was so very very sudden

*really wasn't it? Too terribly sudden. Yet, looking
back it is better, because he wouldn't like to be ill.
No. I don't remember him ill. I remember seven
years of Gretta's illness, and what's more, a dete-
rioration of the mind. But we never saw him ill.
That last week Robert was alive. I never saw him
so active mentally."*

"*I can honestly say that there was something
deeper worrying Robert (sobs) because he would
get into passions of temper with me. If a problem
was worrying him, in London, I used to know that
he wouldn't sleep. He couldn't sleep. He would
work out his problems at night so I knew that Robert was worried about something. He was anxious,
and if I'd say to him like this 'What's worrying
you, Robert?' I could only get an answer if I put
my arm round him. So I never asked that question
unless I was very near to him. Otherwise he would
get into terrible tempers, and so I began not to ask
him. This went on practically from our second visit
away. So I'm positively certain that something must
have happened. Aunt Gretta had been speaking
about her will a lot, and you know very well I
never would listen to wills. I hated anybody talking about wills. Robert also had a habit of talking
about wills. When he was going away, if the war
was going to come, and everything else, he would
always be pre-thinking for us. I was younger and I
would not listen. One afternoon that last week,
Robert locked the doors, came down and he tried to
talk. He was saying; if anything happened to him
I would be all right (very tiredly). The Monday
before he died . . . he died on the Saturday . . . the
Monday before he died, he said to me that I would
be all right.*"

Now Robert was gone. Edna after nearly forty
years of companionship was left alone.

227

Chapter 13

Emigration and Back

Edna missed Robert badly.

"In the first years it was terribly hard, terribly hard. Nobody knows. It still is hard. No, no. I wouldn't have been wiser to move away. No. You would never have stopped missing him. What upset me more than anything . . . One of the worst things: Jean, fair play, and Gwyn took me to Rhoson-Sea. But I couldn't see a man and woman walk, if that man had white hair and the woman was my age, without fretting."

"I think my salvation has been my second grandchild, the birth of my second grandchild so soon afterwards. And the HAVING to drive that car. There have been times when I haven't known what to do. There still come times I don't know

what to do (crying). I don't think moving will do it. I sometimes feel like getting away, from 'Maesnewydd'. But I don't think it will help me. I don't think it will ever help me. It's terribly lonely . . . I see him everywhere . . . I don't think I would have got over it only being in the garden, in the garden . . ."

One main difficulty for a widow, apart from missing her life's companion, is the inability to take the reigns of her life simply because she has never had the chance to drive her own chariot before. If she has had a career before then it can be re-established, but in Edna's case as for millions of other woman, this was not possible.

"If I could have changed one thing earlier in life to help me later, I would have finished my training. I'm sorry to this day I never finished my training, because it is a job in your hand. Every woman ought to have some qualifications whereby she can be independent if necessary. There comes a time even in the best of marriages . . . there's no marriage yet, that to my mind, can be all good times. And if there is a disagreement, or rather an adjustment of one's ideas to the other's . . . to the other party's . . . whereby it is better for both to be independent, and have independent thoughts, it is better for the woman to be able to stand alone. Well, in my life, that sort of attitude was impossible. In my life there was nothing of that. I was overruled in whatever I said. Women's emancipation hadn't come you see. Yes, oh yes, The woman always depended on the husband."

It was amazing that Edna felt this way. She was one of the older generations of wives; those brought up to respect and follow any husband. AND she had had a remarkably happy marriage, and in her widowhood she missed her husband desperately. Yet she could feel this way about the necessity for woman to be able to stand equal when necessary. Now she needed a job and was not qualified.

She had tried to get a job before.

"63 years . . . it's a fair old time yes. My life has been very happy, but very busy . . . very happy and very busy. The happiest time was when we married and we began to rear the children, as far as I was concerned. You see 1926 until the children were . . . until the children left home. Then I was terribly 'digalon' (unhappy) . . . after they went I didn't know what to do with myself. I began to be discontented. In fact, I applied to Brynberyl Hospital. I went for an interview. After the youngest, John, went to college, I went to Caernarvon and I was interviewed by a doctor. I was told to await an application from the matron but I never had it. The doctor in Caernarvon said that I was quite all right and 'they would be delighted to use you'. I knew I was going only to get a job in the wards it was. Well, it so happened that summer time came along and while I was waiting for a letter from the matron of the hospital . . . they changed the matrons. They changed the matron to a Llithfaen matron. I didn't get the job and I'm sorry now. It would have been very good indeed and I was quite willing to go on night duty because Robert said 'I'll drive you there and drive you back.' But he was only half hearted really about it."

Meanwhile she was still very useful to her relatives at 'Maesnewydd' and they could use her help . . . though without pay! So she managed 'Wal-

Cum' with its garden and chickens, and lived on her police and old-age pensions for the next few years. Her driving became renowned in the area. After a first driving test failure, necessity drove her to success and she took up the car independently at age 63. Of course, being an ex-Metropolitan Crime Chief's widow she was well known to the local Caernarvonshire constabulary. In addition, the Caernarvonshire County Chief Constable had been in school with her, and since he was now a widower, they became friendly once more. Finally, she became a spokeswoman for the National of Retired Police Officers (NARPO), an association in which Robert had once served as Secretary. These three facts gave Edna virtual immunity from the police . . . especially with respect to her driving!

Roads are narrow in Britain and narrower in Wales. Around Pwllheli a 12-foot width was a TWO-lane highway, and since there are no 'shoulders' it was common to squeeze past an oncoming car while narrowly brushing the adjacent hedge. Edna brushed them rather violently on occasions and her little yellow Ford Anglia had numerous side scratches and dents that appeared in, to her, a most mysterious fashion. When she parked in town on market days she was able to ignore all parking restrictions, leaving the yellow car on any convenient corner, since she said: 'Oh, they know me.' Sure enough the police would look after her, sometimes moving the car to a safer area but then waiting around to tell her, on her return from shopping, where it was.

As age increased, Edna occasionally fell and on one occasion she lay on the path outside the backdoor without assistance for an hour. It became more serious. Her son John and his wife, Claire, felt it would be better if she sold out and came to live with his family in the US, since his sister had died a few years before. What was not realized by anyone, was that this not only meant care for Edna, but also the loss of independence that she had gained in the past seven years.

Nevertheless, the change was made. He wrote asking her to join their family. She replied:

> *'Your letter of Monday has quite taken my breath away. To be wanted by someone at least is something, but to know there is a place I can come to is wonderful.'* She continued that she felt *'very tempted to come'*, but before the end of the letter she decided . . . *'Yes. I'll come children.'*

'Wal-Cum' was sold (for 12 times it's initial price) and belongings disposed of. Passport, US visa, travel arrangements accomplished. Edna arrived in the US as a green card permanent alien, on January 25, 1972 . . . an immigrant at the age of 71.

The move didn't work . . .

In retrospect it is easy to see why.

At first at least her stay in Monroeville, Pennsylvania was happy enough and she adored her two small grandchildren. Paul aged 7 and Jennifer 4. She was happy enough being taken around to see and experience her new home, and to select furniture for her own living-cum-bedroom room.

With the family she traveled. Some of the happiest times were those in the station-wagon exploring Williamsburg, the Okefenokee and the shoreline around Cape Hattaras. Everyone suffered from the heat and enjoyed the ocean. Grandmother was in her element playing with the children. Back in Pittsburgh, she is remembered for giving piggy-backs and letting the children play house with her collection of Hummel figures! But these activities proved to be the shine on life rather than the quality of her life itself.

Edna had been independent for a decade. Yet her son, John offered her security and care, which, although they didn't realize it, deprived her of any need to do anything. She was expected to be a quiet unobtrusive Grandmother 'sitting quietly by the fireside knitting'. She had her own living quarters but she was not about to be put out to pasture in her remaining days. She was now used to living her own recognizance, doing for herself, making her own mind up . . . she was not a passive helpless individual. First and foremost she wanted to drive again.

Unfortunately, she took too active an interest in the management of the grandchildren. The situation got worse. Each evening, John would return from work to a household in turmoil: his wife in tears, his mother in tears and his children in tears. It took an evening to sort out. The problem was invariably a dispute over what was best for the children: whether, for example, they were allowed to play with their friends on the late summer evening or whether they had to come in to bed. Mother and Grandmother disagreed and acted upon their own beliefs. It came to an 'either-she-goes-or-I-go' ultimatum.

The solution appeared to be a separate apartment for Edna close by, to increase her independent life and cut the dual authority in the house. Unfortunately, when all was arranged, she refused to go.

In those days everyone was under stress. Claire suffered headaches. John developed an ulcer and Edna had terrible migraines and periods of irrationality. These periods often resulted in her wanting to phone the police at night for protection (she always trusted any policeman), or speaking incoherently, or even rolling, on the floor in mental turmoil. It was not known then, neither did doctors diagnose her problem much later. It is probable even then that she was suffering micro-strokes (capillary bleeding in the brain) brought on by stress. It is a sad reflection on our medical knowledge that we have, for so long, ascribed such a physical disability to mental deficiency . . . and even then treat this as a matter of shame rather than of sickness. At that time Edna's condition was not even suspected.

The situation was so uncomfortable that in Britain, Maria already suspected a return was possible. She said later:

> "I told Emrys too, about Edna. 'Now look here Emrys'. I said 'if Edna comes over here from America, she's not going to wander around Pwllheli. She's got to come here into this house. I'm going look after her.' You see, and he never said a word against it. He knew, you see, that that was the right thing to do."

However Edna had no intention of returning to Britain.

Just when the position had become almost intolerable and it was possible that the family might even break up under the strain, Emrys, Edna's brother died. She left for the funeral and she was encouraged to stay in Britain to live with sister Maria, who was now left alone after Emrys's death. This was an excuse to resolve an ugly problem, and the relationship between Edna and her son, John, was very poor.

Edna justifiably felt that she had been offered a home and then thrown back, now without the security of her old home. She arrived back on May 28, 1973, after 16 months in the United States. Letters thereafter were venomous. It took a year to resolve and to clear deeply hurt feelings.

Chapter 14

Final Years

It was a sad time for all concerned. Human relationships exist only in the mind, but they can be as real as being struck by a fist or stroked by compassionate fingers.

Edna's letters reflected her confused turmoil. Half-finished sentences, half-started thoughts, anger, sorrow and hurt, all exposed in anguished scrawl. The distance and time compounded the agony. John felt at a loss. Closeness would have allowed a touch and arm around the shoulders held tight, but 3,000 miles requires the use of very inadequate words. He never was able to explain that although harm had been done, Edna's return to live in Britain was probably the best solution.

Edna, however, was a ship adrift. She was set down

in Pwllheli, her old hometown, without a home to go to. Strangers occupied 'Wal-Cum' The only sanctuary was 'Maesnewydd' and her sister Maria. Maria too was alone now that Emrys had died, and from a distance it looked a perfect solution. The two sisters could find comfort and support from each other. They had always got on well together. The house, set in farmland looking across the fields to the coast at Afonwen, was quiet but well served by buses and neighbours.

However, it didn't work quite so well! Maria welcomed her sister to her home to live, but Edna saw 'Maesnewydd' as it had been before — someone else's home, not hers. She could not think of living there in companionship with her sister. She wanted her independence and a 'place of her own'. So even while she was staying at 'Maesnewydd' she never entirely settled.

Correspondence between Edna and her son, John, remained rancorous for months. She blamed him for 'sending her back to Britain'. This was in part correct, because the situation had become so impossible. However, time heals wounds and they slowly became friends again. It looked as though Edna and Maria might settle in a few more months.

They did for a time live happily in Chwilog. Though Edna never drove again. Ria had a car so they were mobile and could visit the town. Edna worked in the 'Maesnewydd' garden and audio-tapes from the pair showed that they were no different than before. Edna was still the domineering force although Ria could show considerable persistence when she wanted her own way.

However, Edna's health worsened, and she began to fall again, and require more attention than

Ria could give. Then Edna had a partial stroke, and was confined to bed as Gretta had been before her. She knew so well how debilitating a stroke was and how inhumane it could be for the patient. When John visited her, she was at death's door. She could hardly move her arms and her speech was slurred and colour non-existent. Still after his visit she improved, rose and finally was able to walk without impairment. She still had excruciating headaches as she had had in the US, and the doctors she attended never diagnosed these.

After that she needed more care, and they, Edna and Ria, decided she would get it better in a nursing home. Edna then moved to Plas Havan (The Haven) in Pwllheli, a rather sad very modern group of buildings occupied by pastured old men and women. Photographs showed her sitting with them on a long bench in the sun outside a concrete wall.

The headaches got very much worse, and incoherence and apparent mental incapability accompanied them. Everyone had Willie in mind. Edna wrote:

> "*I was taken to see a psychiatrist a week ago in Bangor and he said in my presence 'I can see nothing wrong', so please help me to get out (of Plas Havan.)*'"

And later

> "*Well, I am being driven to madness. I am in what is half of the old Medical Hospital. I still know where I am, and why, I am quite all right . . . please write to me because I am disturbed mentally . . .*"

Yet the truth was that the headaches were symptomatic of minor capillary ruptures in the brain: ministrokes, which affected the brain in a very physical way. During the worst attacks Edna became incoherent and needed someone present so that she would not hurt herself. She had to be protected and she felt the confinement. She wrote:

> *"As soon as I can, if you won't get me out, I'll find the policeman and they will get me out or else I'll walk out."*

She still trusted the policeman above all else.

Eventually it was clear she needed full hospital care. Then the worst happened. The hospital selected was Denbigh! All youngsters in North Wales know 'Denbigh' as the insane asylum. They joke about it as insane asylums are joked of everywhere. To the Morgans, Denbigh had a special meaning because Willie had been incarcerated there for 25 years, never to emerge. It was a place in which the patient had NO say whatsoever. No matter that in the intervening years, Denbigh had been rehabilitated into a more normal hospital dealing with the physically, as well as mentally, sick. Edna knew where she had been taken. That knowledge, in itself, was a sentence.

Her letters became disjointed, almost a random collection of words. Yet among them were glimpses of serenity in a disordered mind. In a scrawl of disjointed half-thought she said:

> *"I have a letter to answer one of yours but I have to answer one of yours and read yours first.*

*The best bit of news is your your news is that your
news is your yours your going to rest a while.*"

. . . And yet in the very middle of similar chaos
she says:

*"It's time we women had some laurels. Robert
always had a Police stripe.*"

She did come out of Denbigh for a short time
after fighting improvement, but was taken back as
the attacks continued. This time she never emerged,
and she slowly sank into an unresponsive stillness.

When John visited her, she lay connected to tubes
to clear the fluid from her throat. Her eyes fixed
unseeing in the distance. There was no sign that she
knew anyone was with her, that anyone spoke, or that
anyone touched her. There was no sign of thought
or understanding. Was she inwardly living her past,
romping down the beach at Towyn, or running
around the builder's materials in the back yard? Was
she reliving times with Robert, toiling on the garden, in North Wales, and taking her children for
walks? It was a comfort to feel that old people retreat vividly to past years, and see them more clearly
than yesterday. If thought existed then it was probably happily remembering times 50 years earlier.

There was no communication. All that was possible was a touch or two in the hope that it was felt.

Edna died on August 5th 1978, aged 77 years

Epilogue

What measure of success can you place on a life? Edna was not a suffragette, nor an initiator on behalf of others. She tried to take advantage of her own opportunities and within the social bounds of the day she raised her family. She had failures and successes. Her failure to become a career nurse measured the social restrictions of the day. Her success in raising a family and overcoming widowhood mirrored the successes of thousands of other women, and measured the social allowances of the day.

Another woman in her time and age would have been subjected to the same social pressures and restrictions. Readers may recognize their Mothers. Women of later ages will recognize the bounds, which have been lifted, and the degrees by which men and women are now subject to the same bounds. There will be no age when there are no social pressures . . . they change, and indeed they could become even greater as populations increase.

There is an Italian proverb . . . that a man has not lived unless he has built a house, written a book or begotten a child. Edna lived.

She told her son:

> *"I'll tell you this. I'm very very glad too that I've got grandchildren to keep me alive. If I had only my children I think that I would be very despondent about it all. I feel that now I have grandchildren . . . while we have grandchildren we never die. Daddy nor Mummy ever dies. Because I feel with Jean . . . when Jean was alive I could see traces of my Mother. I could also see traces of Father in Jean. I can see traces of my Father in you, and I can see, in Paul, already traces of Daddy. I can see traces of quickness there. And I don't think we really die when the family is perpetuated."*

Edna Graham
Weymouth, England.
1967

The Principal Line of
the Morgans Family

(1) John MORGANS
& Jane Clocker
m. 22 Jan 1813, Llanbadernfawr, Wales

(2) John MORGANS
& Elizabeth Margaretta MORGAN
b. 1 Oct 1822, Cynnullmawr, Wales
d. 26 Feb 1879, St Cadvans, Towyn, Meirionyddshire, Wales
m. 24 Mar 1852, Llanfihangel Geneur Glyn, Landre, Caernaerfonshire

(3) Thomas MORGANS
& Jane JONES
b. 6 Apr 1863, Fford Derfyn, Rhuddlan, Denbigh
d. 3 Nov 1931, Maesnewydd, Towyn, Meirionyddshire, Wales
m. 19 Sep 1887, Gaston, Derbyshire, England

(4) Edna MORGANS
& Robert William GRAHAM
b. 18 Dec 1890, Lunnon, Nenthead, Cumberland
d. 4 Apr 1964, Pwllheli, Caernarvonshire, Wales
m. 24 Oct 1925, Bethesda Congregational Church, Towyn, Meirionydd

(5) Jean GRAHAM
& Edward Gwyn MORRIS
b. 1924
m. 1952, Pwllheli, Caernarvonshire, Wales

(6) Robert Edward Clive MORRIS
& Rita Morris
b. 1951, Malta
m. 1994

(7) Robert George MORRIS

(7) Jean Elizabeth MORRIS

(5) John Graham
& Claire Esmeralda BIGGERSTAFF
b. 3 Apr 1934, Old Street, London
m. 12 Jul 1958, Muswell Hill, London, England

(6) Paul GRAHAM

(6) Jennifer GRAHAM
& John Paul Leeming
b. 8 Apr 1967, Redlands, California, USA
m. 7 Aug 1989, Anchorage, Alaska, U.S.A.

(7) Ian Angus Leeming

(5) John Graham
& Emmy (Mieke) Liliane Adrienne Roos
b. 13 Jan 1969, Hoogstraten, Belgium
m. 13 Dec 1996, Golden, Colorado, USA

243

A Woman's Times

In the first decades of the 20th century a woman's life at home was spent principally in keeping things clean. This included the house, linens, clothes, children, and sometimes even the husband. The time spent in feeding and caring for the family in other ways was a relatively smaller proportion of her time.

Washing the family linen and clothing took a full two days of her week, if not more. In the poorer homes there was insufficient clothing to make frequent changes unless it was also washed frequently, so that there might be two or more washings a week. Each was a back breaking effort with fires for boilers to be lit and cared for, water to be carried for boilers, wet clothes to be handled in 'clouds of steam', hand mangling to be done before the clothes could be carried out and hung on the line. Then they were gathered, folded and ironed before being ready for use. The main wash of the week took at least a day and a half, and together with another smaller wash day, this was about 35% of her life.

Added to this there were dishes and pans to be washed and dried, rooms to be dusted, windows to be washed, cutlery to be polished, and floors and door steps to be scrubbed. Most of this was manual labor, using water, soap and elbow grease.

In between the woman shopped for, or grew food, cleaned and prepared it, cooked and served it, and looked after the husband and the children.

Thus, spare time to read, to talk with others, and to form her opinions on the state of the country and the world, was fairly limited. A vote was of no use to the working woman.

The industrial revolution in the 1800s was more than a period of economic growth for the industrialized nations: it was a time of liberation for the woman in the home. Many of the inventions then were later to reduce the amount of time that a woman spent in the cycle of unproductive labor. They eventually allowed her time to think about other things in life.

The date of an invention is of only academic interest, since typically there are many years between the invention and its practical use. For example, the Swiss Audemars had discovered rayon in 1855, and yet it was not used until 1912 when rayon stockings were sold. Its general use, and even its naming, was delayed until 1925. Similarly although Bell invented the telephone in 1876, the first New York telephone exchange didn't open until 1892. Edna still couldn't use one in 1923 and didn't have one in 'Wal-Cum' until about 1960. Marconi invented the radio in 1896 but it didn't get into general use until 1920. The radio amateurs of the early twenties were ahead of the state of the art. On average, the time between invention and development for the public was 20 to 25 years.

However, even when such innovations were made, those women that really could have made use of them, typically were not those able to afford to do so. Thus, there was a further delay before the appliances came down in price sufficiently for general use. Since the clothes wringer was invented in 1865, refinements of this hand-wound device were still in general use until after World War II, even though electric wringers and electric dryers were 'invented' about the same time as the electric washing machine in 1907. The electric flat iron, invented in 1882, and the electric sewing machine of 1889 were luxuries for women even thirty years later.

These two delays, development and the reduction in price, must be taken into account in reading the following chronology. When Edna entered nursing and went into service the labor saving devices that existed were almost all-mechanical ones. Electric conveniences were not then available, and because of the advent of World War II, it wasn't until the 1950s that they could be obtained. Still in almost all respects her life was easier than that of her Mother . . . there was some time left for her reading in the early years, and for her entertainment and travel in the later years. The car, starting in 1925, was a principal liberator.

For the record, Edna never had a washing machine or dryer, although she had used an electric boiler since 1938.

She did get a refrigerator in about 1957 although before that milk and butter had kept quite well on a marble slab in a cool pantry. Eggs were preserved over winter in isinglass and meat was bought weekly. From the forties, she had electric appliances: stove, kettle, vacuum cleaner, sewing machine and iron.

However she also used a coal-fired range, mechanical carpet sweeper and coal-heated flatiron as reserves. The range in particular was called into service each Sunday for the roast, since it was so much larger than the electric stove. Water for 'Wal-Cum' could be heated by electric immersion heater or from the large cooking range so it was the latter that was generally used. Robert had radios ever since he built his own cat's whiskers crystal sets. They had a hand wound gramophone from the first days of their marriage, but television didn't become cheap enough to be available in Wales until 1952.

Acceptance of the working woman allowed Edna to think of a career first, before marriage. Since from the turn of the century in Britain, women were allowed in certain careers. Political equality for women had little to no effect on her life. She was allowed to vote in 1928, but at that time she was fully engaged with a young and growing family. Then came the war and her husband, Robert's retirement. Thus any signs of growing social equality was masked by her life's set pattern. Her own daughter gained a little by the movement for women's equality, in that it was axiomatic, as it was for her son, that her daughter should go on to college from school. Yet, teaching was still the principal job opening available to women in the 1950's.

Edna was able to handle her own affairs during the later years of Robert's life, and after his death, and contribute to such organizations as the National Association of Retired Police Officers, partly because women then had a new confidence in their own ability. The time was right. However, the technological changes that had eased her life and allowed her time were far more important than any political changes.

Date	Technology	Women's Suffrage	Edna's Milestones
1825	Safety pin (Hunt)		
1844	Telegraph (Morse)		
1846	Sewing machine (Howe)		
1855	Rayon (Audemars)		
1865	Clothes wringer		
1867	Typewriter (Scholes)		
1868	Lawnmower (Hills)		
1872		Male universal ballot (UK)	
1876	Telephone (Bell)		
1879	Electric light (Edison and Swan)		
1882	Electric fan (Wheeler) Electric flatiron (Seely)		
1889	Electric sewing machine (Singer)		
1890		Women's rights agitation	
1896	Radio (Marconi) Electrical stove (Hadaway)		

249

Date	Technology	Women's Suffrage	Edna's Milestones
1899	Vacuum cleaner (Thurmann)		
1901		Queen Victoria dies	Born: Towyn, Wales (Jun 3rd)
1903	Powered flight (Wright brothers)		
1906		Women's suffrage movement becomes active (UK) Susan B. Anthony died	
1907	Electric washing machine (Fisher)		
1909	Cheap cars (Model T) (Henry Ford)	US adopt British women's methods of protest	Brother Jack dies
1910		Florence Nightingale dies	
1911		Washington State allows women voters	
1912	Rayon in general use	California allows women	
	1914-1918 WORLD WAR I		
1918	Electric refrigerators	Votes for women over 30	Nursing (Liverpool)

Date	Technology	Women's Suffrage	Edna's Milstones
1920	Radio in public use	Degrees for women at Oxford University	
1921			In service (London)
1924		19th Amendment passed (USA)	Nursing (London)
1925	Television (Baird & Jenkins)		Married to Robert Graham (Oct 24)
1926	Electric toaster	Women enfranchised	First child: Jean (Aug 10)
1928	Air-condition building		
1933		Emmeline Pankhurst died	Second child: John (Jan 25)
1936	BBC TV Service		
1938	US work week cut		Retirement to Wales
1938-1945 WORLD WAR II			
1947		Schooling to 15 (UK)	Evacuations from London

)-GRAH

Date	Technology	Women's Suffrage	Edna's Milestones
1950	Synthetic materials	Polygamy and child marriages abolished Equal right to both sexes (China)	
	Women's labor week cut (UK)		
1954			Food rationing ends (UK)
1956	Nuclear power (May 23, Calder Hall, UK)		First grandchild: Clive
1957	Electric typewriter	Women vote for first time since 1952 revolution (Egypt)	
1959	Women's labor week cut further (UK)		
1961			Brother William dies
1964	Permanent press materials		Robert Graham dies Second grandchild: Paul
1967			Third grandchild: Jennifer Brother Tom dies

Date	Technology	Women's Suffrage	Edna's Milestones
1968			Son John and family emigrates to US
1971		Sex discrimination in hiring illegal (Wash)	Daughter Jean dies
1972			Emigration to USA
1973			Brother Emrys dies Return to Britain
1975		Equal rights amendment attempted (USA) Discrimination in athletics banned (PA, USA)	
1978			Edna dies (Aug 5), aged 77

253

Index